COURTS AND PROCEDURE IN ENGLAND AND IN NEW JERSEY

BY
CHARLES HOPKINS HARTSHORNE

Published by Left of Brain Books

Copyright © 2021 Left of Brain Books

ISBN 978-1-396-32162-7

First Edition

All rights reserved. No part of this publication may be reproduced, distributed, or transmitted in any form or by any means, including photocopying, recording, or other electronic or mechanical methods, without the prior written permission of the publisher, except in the case of brief quotations embodied in critical reviews and certain other noncommercial uses permitted by copyright law. Left of Brain Books is a division of Left of Brain Onboarding Pty Ltd.

Table of Contents

PREFACE.   1

CHAPTER I. THE PROPOSED CONSTITUTIONAL AMENDMENTS OF 1903. THEIR INADEQUACY.   7

CHAPTER II. THE JUDICIAL SYSTEM OF NEW JERSEY.   10

CHAPTER III. THE COURT SYSTEMS OF THE NEW ENGLAND STATES. GETTING INTO THE WRONG COURT.   16

CHAPTER IV. DOUBLE LITIGATION. THE JUDICIAL SYSTEMS OF OTHER STATES.   21

CHAPTER V. LAW AND EQUITY.   31

CHAPTER VI. HOW TO AVOID DOUBLE LITIGATION IN SINGLE CONTROVERSIES. AMERICAN AND ENGLISH EXPERIENCE.   41

CHAPTER VII. THE ENGLISH SYSTEM OF COURTS AND THEIR JURISDICTION. THE DANGERS FROM DIVIDED JURISDICTIONS.   46

CHAPTER VIII. UNITY AND MULTIPLICITY IN FORMS OF ACTIONS.   56

CHAPTER IX. DEFECTS OF PARTIES.   65

CHAPTER X. WHAT REDRESS DEFENDANT MAY HAVE. SET-OFF, RECOUPMENT, COUNTERCLAIM.   74

CHAPTER XI. SUMMONS, PLEADINGS, DEMURRERS.   79

CHAPTER XII. JUDGMENTS.   86

CHAPTER XIII. APPELLATE PROCEDURE.   90

CHAPTER XIV. ENGLISH EXPERIENCE IN PIECEMEAL REFORM, FROM THE COMMON-LAW AND CHANCERY PROCEDURE ACTS TO THE JUDICATURE ACT.   98

CHAPTER XV. THE PRACTICAL WORKING OF THE ENGLISH JUDICATURE ACTS.   110

CHAPTER XVI. THE PRINCIPLES OF THE ENGLISH PROCEDURE.   119

APPENDIX. 127
    I. Selections From the English Judicature Acts. 127
    II. Selections from the Rules of Court. 138
    III. Suggestions for the Improvement of Our Judicial System. 164

PREFACE.

What I have written in Chapter VI and in the Appendix is first published in this book. All the other chapters were published in the years 1902-1905, as articles in the *New Jersey Law Journal*. They have been somewhat revised. There were two series of these articles; the first, entitled "Antiquated Courts and Miscarriage of Justice," was published prior to the election upon the proposed Constitutional Amendments, which was held in September 1903. The second series, entitled "How Can We Improve Our Judicial System?" was published after the defeat of the Amendments. Chapter I was published as a separate article, between the two series and when the election was impending.[1]

---

[1] The original articles and the dates of their publication were as follows:

Chapter in this book.	No. of article in the series.	In Law Journal of	Name of Series.
II.	1st.	February, 1902.	"Antiquated Courts."
III.	2d.	March, 1902.	"Antiquated Courts."
IV.	3d.	April, 1902.	"Antiquated Courts."
V.	4th.	June, 1902.	"Antiquated Courts."
VI.		Not heretofore published.	
VII.	5th.	September, 1902.	"Antiquated Courts."
VIII.	6th.	October, 1902.	"Antiquated Courts."
IX.	7th.	November, 1902.	"Antiquated Courts."
X.	8th.	February, 1903.	"Antiquated Courts."
XI.	9th.	April, 1903.	"Antiquated Courts."
XII.	10th.	May, 1903.	"Antiquated Courts."
XIII.	11th.	June, 1903.	"Antiquated Courts."
I.		July, 1903.	A separate article, not in either series.
XIV.	1st.	September, 1904,	How Can We Improve Our Judicial System.
XV.	2d.	May, 1905,	How Can We Improve Our Judicial System.
XVI.	3d.	June, 1905,	How Can We Improve Our Judicial System.

After the proposed Amendments were defeated, the State Bar Association, at its annual meeting in June 1904, appointed a committee to try to get legislative authority for a commission to examine, upon broad lines, the subject of the improvement of the judicial system, and to report to the legislature. The resolutions are in the Year Book of the Association (1904), p. 20. The bill prepared by the committee for that purpose was enacted as Chapter 88 of the Laws of 1905, and the commission, appointed by the governor, is now at work. It is an excellent commission and its report will be received upon all sides with respect.[2]

Some of my friends were displeased at the opposition manifested in the first series of articles to the then proposed Amendments. But I thought, and still think, that had these been adopted there would certainly have been no great improvement in our judicature for many years to come. It is most difficult to awaken, among lawyers, a sentiment for reform in legal procedure. Had the Amendments been adopted, the threatened congestion of business in the Supreme court and Court of Appeals, which alarmed the profession and aroused it to action, would have been allayed, temporarily at least, and the bar would have relapsed into slumber. Let him who doubts upon this point inquire what interest the bar has shown during the last half century in any general and systematic improvement of the judicial system. It remains to be seen whether this lethargy is interrupted now.

When the time comes, as come it must, for the reconstruction of our curious old judicial system by a statesmanlike reform, these pages, I hope, will put within the reach of those who wish to know, somewhat of the experience of other communities in attempting to solve the problem that now faces us.

The large discretionary power which should be vested in the courts to control procedure presupposes a bench of able, experienced, and conscientious judges, free from bias and acting under public scrutiny. Such a power should certainly not be given to justices of the peace, in our present vicious system of justices' courts; and perhaps it should be introduced with caution into other inferior courts unless their personnel is considerably

---

[2] The commission consists of Hon. John W. Griggs, Hon. Franklyn Murphy, Hon. Bennet Van Syckel, Charles L. Corbin, Esq., John R. Hardin, Esq.

improved. Upon the whole, our state has been fortunate in the kind of men selected as judges for the superior courts. If the average personnel of the county courts is not as satisfactory, it is at all events far better than it was a generation ago when the local judges of these courts were laymen. The improvement of our judicial organization and procedure is a very important reform, but it is not nearly as important as is the maintenance of the character of our superior judiciary and the raising of the character of the inferior. The best system of procedure counts for little, of course, in the absence of character, ability, independence, fearlessness, and expert training, upon the bench. That we have those qualities now in the members of the superior courts is due, in large measure, to the custom of re-appointing the judges as their respective terms expire. A judge of the Supreme Court or Court of Chancery, once appointed, may be reasonably sure of retaining his seat as long as he is able to do his official work, if he does it well. Unhappily this custom does not extend, in full force, to appointments to the inferior courts, though it is, perhaps, growing in strength even in respect to them.

Fortunately we have escaped, thus far, the curse of an elective judiciary and the scandals that, in our system of politics, are pretty sure, sooner or later, to grow upon it. Impairment of the dignity of the courts and a lessening of public confidence in them are the sure fruits of such scandals. I cannot conceive an advantage in having judges nominated by an irresponsible party boss instead of a responsible governor. With us, it is idle to talk of the people choosing their judges by the elective system. They may do so, but generally they do not. The bald fact is that the people ratify, generally, one of two opposing nominations, good or bad, made respectively by two opposing bosses and their advisers. Rare exceptions to that rule occur when some scandalous party action in refusing a re-nomination that ought to be made or in making an especially offensive nomination, shocks public sentiment into active, organized opposition. Short of that extreme, the bosses may fill the bench with politicians who do not cease to be partisans when they become judges. Doubtless there are many other exceptions to the rule; but who wishes such a rule to be established here for the selection of judges? A powerful interest may, and indeed, sometimes does, influence a governor to make a bad nomination, but how much more easily the same interest may influence a boss.

Since the days of Bentham and Austin the distinction has been well recognized, in theory, between substantive law and adjective law; that is, between the law which defines the substantive rights of life, of liberty, of status, and of property, and the law by which there is created and operated the machinery for the protection of those substantive rights.[3] The latter is generally called the law of adjective rights. In this book it is called the law of procedure. Not much practical use, however, has heretofore been made of the distinction between these two great divisions.

If we look into the law of procedure for principles which are essential and not accidental, which arise from the nature of legal rights, and not from the arbitrary *fiat* of the lawgiver or the chance growth of a custom, it seems to me that they should be summarized thus:

1. The right to have the matter in question decided by a court of competent jurisdiction. Otherwise, a self-constituted tribunal could usurp the power to sit in judgment upon my legal rights. In the orderly administration of public justice, the judicial function can be derived from the supreme power of the state only.[4]

2. The right to a fair opportunity to be heard. This implies the right—

(*a*) To formal notice of judicial action; and,

(*b*) To a reasonable opportunity to present to the court the evidence and arguments of the parties relevant to the matter in question.

Upon this right it is necessary to impose many limitations which cannot be considered here. The kind of judicial notice and of opportunity for hearing to be given must differ with the nature and situation of the matter in question; instance the seizure of a ship in admiralty, the foreclosure of a mortgage, damages for a personal injury. But in a civilized state, no system of procedure

---

[3] For a definition of substantive and adjective law, consult Holland, "Elements of Jurisprudence," pp. 147, 315. Austin calls the divisions "Primary" and "Secondary" law. "Lectures on Jurisprudence" (Campbell's ed.), 1032.

[4] In New Jersey the legislature cannot legalize a judicial act void for want of jurisdiction. Maxwell *v.* Gœtschius, 40 N. J. L. 383.

would be endured which did not purport to safeguard the right to a fair opportunity to be heard, upon judicial notice.[5]

3. *The right to have the court render judgment upon the matter (issues) presented by the parties.*

If the parties try only the question whether one is liable in damages for an injury done to the person of the other, the court cannot convict of the crime of assault and give judgment of imprisonment, even though it have both civil and criminal jurisdiction.[6]

4. *The right to have the court award, by its judgment, the kind of remedy or relief which it is authorized by law to award in the matter in question.*

A court having power to enforce its judgment by seizure and sale of property only, cannot issue a warrant of arrest, or a writ of injunction, or of mandamus. To do so would be to exceed its jurisdiction.[7]

These four rights I call *essential* rights; for they are essential to the protection of substantive rights. They differ in nature from the numberless adjective rights which depend upon laws prescribing the details of procedure; such as the right to sue or be sued in this or that form of action, the right to security for costs, and the like. The latter are non-essential to the protection of substantive rights. They are, for the most part, mere regulations of convenience for the orderly presentation and investigation of the case. The former are constitutional rights; they cannot be impaired by the legislature. The latter may be given and withdrawn by the legislature at will.

These essential rights should be safeguarded by law, or by law and by legally authorized rules of court. If those safeguards be substantially violated in any case, the proceeding should be arrested or annulled as the circumstances of the case may require; and that, even though the substantive rights in controversy be left undetermined. But a system of procedure which, in any ordinary action, compels a superior court to dismiss the parties with their controversy unsettled, no safeguard of an essential right having been violated, ought not

---

[5] That due process of law requires judicial notice to be given is now a familiar elemental rule. Pennoyer *v.* Neff, 95 U. S. 727. It is equally necessary that the parties have an opportunity to be heard. Windsor *v.* McVeigh, 93 U. S. 274; Roller *v.* Holly, 176 U. S. 399.

[6] A judgment entirely outside the issue made upon the record is void. Munday *v.* Vail, 34 N. J. L. 418; Reynolds *v.* Stockton, 140 U. S. 254.

[7] Tweed *v.* Liscomb, 60 N. Y. 559.

to be tolerated in a civilized state. Every slip or mistake in ordinary procedure which does not violate one of these rights should be excusable, in judicial discretion. Courts exist to settle controversies upon the substantive and essential rights of the people; and there must be something wrong in a system which compels the judges to sacrifice these rights or to delay the settlement of them needlessly, in order to determine non-essential details of procedure.

Questions of procedure must arise and be settled. But they may be divided into two classes those the decision of which may defeat or delay the action; and those which may be determined without delaying it. The problem is to devise a judicial system which shall give rise to as few questions as possible of the former class and provide for a speedy decision of them, while affording adequate safeguards for essential and substantive rights. I think that the English have come nearer the solution of this problem than we Americans, and in this book I have tried to show the principles which they have followed in attempting to solve it.

MONTCLAIR, N. J.   C. H. H.
August, 1905.

CHAPTER I.

THE PROPOSED CONSTITUTIONAL AMENDMENTS OF 1903. THEIR INADEQUACY.[1]

We have a curiously interesting system of courts and procedure. Its fundamental architecture is English of the fourteenth and fifteenth centuries. We have at sundry times torn out great sections of the old building and, piece by piece, have added wings and "lean-tos," so that the whole structure is now very quaint and picturesque indeed. Note what the names suggest: Court of Quarter Sessions, Court of Oyer and Terminer, Court of Common Pleas, Orphans' court, Circuit court, Supreme court, Prerogative court, Court of Chancery, Court of Errors and Appeals. Mark the contrast in Massachusetts, where the list is: Supreme court, Superior court, county Courts of Probate and Insolvency, and that is all, above the municipal courts. You must be careful how you walk in these our halls of justice, for if, by mistake, you enter one with a legal controversy which belongs to another, you will be ejected and fined in costs. Some of them, too, have different entrances for different kinds of cases, and it is deemed of essential importance that in bringing this case you enter by this door, and, with that case, that door. If you mistake in your choice, you will be mulcted in costs and perhaps turned out or compelled to retrace your steps. This, by force of the ancient traditions which have governed our craft since the days of the Edwards, kings of England. But the structure and its traditions, so interesting to antiquarians, are somewhat inconvenient for the uses of the twentieth century. Until recently these inconveniences were experienced only by suitors. They waited while the lawyers disputed before the judges, for months or years, through which door or into which court the controversy ought to have been carried. A century ago

---

[1] This chapter was published in the N. J. LAW JOURNAL of July, 1903, under the title, "The Lawyers and the Constitutional Amendments." Chapters II to XIII, inclusive, except VI, had then been previously published in the series, "Antiquated Courts." The amendments referred to in it were those submitted to the people in the election of September, 1903. They were defeated.

people had time for such delays. While it was only the suitors who waited, we lawyers did not deem the inconvenience unbearable, for in the settlement of these points of procedure—very interesting to us—we found much to do, and on the dicision of each point costs accrued to the lawyers on both sides, the only question being which of the opposing litigants must pay them. In the phrase of Wall street, there was an "active market." But recently, our business has accumulated so fast that it threatens congestion in the Court of Appeals. We may have to wait for a hearing in all our cases, including those which, to the surprise of the litigant on the one side and to the consternation of his opponent, we have made to turn upon these latent and interesting points of procedure. Our clients must wait, too; but if that were all, it is probable that we could endure it. We do not complain when, upon a prompt hearing, the Court of Appeals decides that we began in the wrong court, that our client must pay costs and begin over again. Who thinks of a constitutional amendment to stop that delay? But if *we* must wait, as well as our clients, it will indeed become intolerable. So our State Bar Association has determined to make a reform by a constitutional amendment. True, we have not gone about it in a very statesmanlike way. We have made no inquiry respecting the great tide of judicial reform that has swept over America, England and her colonies within the last century. "What have we to do with abroad?" And, in respect to legal procedure, every place beyond New York and Pennsylvania is "abroad" to us lawyers. It seemed to be much simpler to add another lean-to to our judicial structure. We want a new court, a new Court of Appeals. It is true that neither the United States nor any other state in the Union, except New York, has a Court of Appeals above its Supreme court. It is also true that New Jersey has more kinds of courts than any other state. But our present courts do not suffice to decide our lawsuits promptly—which is small wonder, seeing that our procedure sometimes requires two or three suits to settle one controversy or, by dint of our dexterous tripping of each other's steps, compels the courts often to hear a single controversy several times. I have collected, in a series of articles in the Law Journal, over fifty reported cases in illustration of such doings, merely as instances of classes of other like cases. Travelers sometimes ask why we do not simplify our judicial system and even tell us that in remote countries, like Connecticut, Canada, England, and Australia, these problems of simplifying ancient procedure have been solved in statesmanlike reforms in which the mistakes of hasty states, like New York, have been avoided and which are found satisfactory after a quarter century's use. But most of us are agreed that such reforms cannot be successful. It is, *a priori*, impossible. Then, too, those regions are too remote to interest us. Look over the river at the procedure in New York! And finally, after all, the costs of these delays do not fall upon us. So let us ask the people to give us a new court. It will create five new judgeships, each of which ought to carry a salary of twelve to fifteen thousand dollars; for the judges of the inferior Supreme court get nine thousand, and the state will save the cost ($12,000 or $15,000) of the present Court of Appeals.

CHAPTER II.

The Judicial System of New Jersey.

Our system of courts at present is the most antiquated and intricate that exists in any considerable community of English-speaking people. Inherent in the cumbersome plan of tribunals is a system of procedure quite as antiquated and far more intricate. Both courts and procedure were brought here from England by our colonial forefathers and were worked into a shape fitted to the needs of a rural community of Eighteenth century colonists. They are fundamentally in that shape to-day. Meantime the people of the state have become a great industrial and commercial community, yet there has been no change in the plan of the judicial machinery corresponding to the enormous change in the volume and character of the work which the new conditions of the people bring upon it. Important reforms in details there have been, but, though we have patched the machinery and altered or added a shaft or a wheel here and there, it is still an Eighteenth century provincial mill built upon an English model of the Middle Ages.

The people of the state maintain their courts to settle their legal controversies, yet no suitor can be sure in any case, when his lawyer brings the controversy into court, that it will be settled in that suit. After months or years of legal combat his suit may be dismissed because it was brought in this court instead of that, though both were civil courts of general jurisdiction, held by judges abundantly competent to determine the case upon its merits. During nine successive terms of the Court of Appeals five cases were dismissed by that court on that ground, and in four of the five the Court of Appeals reversed the decree of the court below on that ground.[1]

Or a litigant having a just and lawful defense may find that the court in which he is sued must give judgment against him, because it has no authority to consider that particular defense. Then he must begin a new suit in a second

---

[1] The cases are—Slockbower *v.* Kanouse. 50 N. J. Equity, 481; Beekman *v.* Cottrell, 51 id. 337; Pyatt *v.* Lyons, 51 id. 308; Kean *v.* Union Water Co., 52 id. 813; Bernz *v.* Marcus Sayre Co., 52 id. 275.

court to prevent the first from enforcing against him a judgment which would deprive him of his lawful rights. Or the suitor may find at the outset that, in order to settle the controversy, he must bring two different and successive lawsuits in different courts. For example, if my neighbor and I dispute the question whether he has the right to drive his wagon at his pleasure across my lot, I must bring one suit in one court to prove that he has no such right, and, having obtained judgment in that, I must then bring another suit in another court to prevent him from violating the right by driving across the lot. And either suit may, at any time, be set back to the initial stage, or even come to a futile end, upon the sudden appearance of some hidden flaw in the legal procedure by which is raised a technical question of no interest to any one in the world except the lawyers and judges of this state.

No human knowledge or wisdom suffices to insure against these technical flaws. For whether or not they exist, depends sometimes upon subtle legal distinctions upon which the court below may hold one opinion and the Court of Appeals another; and on which, moreover, an infinite series of Appellate courts might well hold an infinite series of differing opinions.

I think that it must have been New Jersey to which Lord Coleridge, Chief Justice of England, pointed when he said, "I am told there is a state in this progressive Union in which they" (the subtleties of the ancient procedure) "are at this moment as alive as ever, and I venture, therefore, upon this subject to make you a practical suggestion." (Then, after referring to the reservation by Americans of a great National Park, the speaker continued): "Could it not be arranged that, with the sanction of the state itself, some one state should be preserved as a kind of pleading park, in which the glories of the negative pregnant, pleas giving express color, absque hoc, the replication de injuria, rebutter and surrebutter, and all the other weird and fanciful creations of the pleader's brain might be preserved for future ages to gratify the respectful curiosity of your descendants; and that our good old English judges, if ever they revisit the glimpses of the moon, might have some place where their weary souls might rest—some place where they might still find the form preferred to the substance, the statement to the thing stated." (Lord Coleridge's address (1883), N. Y. State Bar Assn. Reports, Vol. 7, p. 39.)

England, whence we inherited these medievalisms, and many of her self-governing colonies and many of the older states of this Union have had, at some time in their history, substantially similar judicial systems of the antiquated pattern which we still retain, and substantially the same medieval procedure. Precisely such abuses as I have pointed out caused prolonged investigations in England, and successful reforms there and in her colonies and in some American states.

Every English-speaking community (with the possible exception of a few of the smaller colonies whose judicial systems I have not examined) has now a simpler system of courts than that to which our lawyers cling with superstitious reverence; and England and most of her self-governing colonies and far the greater number of our states have simpler methods of procedure. New York alone, among those that have made these reforms, has gone to such extravagant lengths in recent years as to over-shoot the mark and to bring into her procedure a worse confusion than she had expelled by earlier and wiser reforms. This remark applies only to her procedure. Her system of courts is simple and excellent.

[In these circumstances our State Bar Association some two years ago (in 1900) appointed a committee of eminent lawyers to advise amendments to the plan of our constitutional judiciary. One might have expected that the committee would ascertain the experience of other Anglo Saxon communities which had made reforms in a system of administering justice substantially common to them and to us, and would have reported, in the light of that information, some moderate measure which would remedy the worst abuses, and give us the benefit of the tried and successful reforms of other states and countries using Anglo-Saxon law. The committee did nothing of the sort. Not a word nor a comment did it offer upon any other attempt at reform. For aught that it tells us, there might as well have been no advance in the administration of justice outside of our own state; nor, for that matter, any delay or miscarriage of justice within it. The committee did not propose to abolish a single unnecessary court, not a single mischievous form of procedure. It proposed to substitute a new Court of Appeals for an old Court of Appeals, and to add one more class of cases to those which may be appealed. That is the extent of the committee's reforms. Other provisions are added in its proposals, but they are subsidiary and of little interest to any save lawyers and judges.

Many advantages, we are told, will follow the proposed changes if they are adopted. A clumsy Court of Appeals will be succeeded by a court of smaller number and of higher average ability. The present Appellate court sits at long intervals; the new court will sit continuously while there is business for it to do. The former, for want of time, is believed to give scant attention to some cases; the latter will have ample time for adequate consideration of all cases.

All that may be true, but there is no need for either court. The Supreme court is abundantly competent to be the court of last resort. Is not the Supreme court of the United States a court of last resort? All other states in the Union, except New York, are satisfied to have a Supreme court perform that function. That court is the one institution which every other state has preserved, with sedulous care, at the head of its judicial system.]

New Jersey and Massachusetts have about the same area, seven thousand eight hundred and fifteen and eight thousand three hundred and fifteen square miles, respectively. The former is divided into twenty-one counties, the latter into fourteen. New Jersey has a population of eighteen hundred thousand; Massachusetts of twenty-eight hundred thousand (census of 1900), and their wealth in 1890 was, for the former, one billion four hundred and forty-five million; for the latter, two billion eight hundred and three million. The following is a comparison of their judicial systems above the grade of municipal courts:[2]

NEW JERSEY.

Names of Courts.	No. of Courts.		No. of Judges.	Compensation of Judges.
Errors and Appeals.	1	Held by justices of Supreme court and Chancellor and 6 special judges	6	$13,000
Chancery.	1	Held by Chancellor and 6 Vice Chancellors	7	64,000
Prerogative	1	Held by Chancellor and one Vice Chancellor called the "Ordinary" and "Vice Ordinary"	...	...

---

[2] The table of judges and judicial salaries was made up in 1902. Since then the salaries have been somewhat increased in both states. Two vice-chancellors and one Circuit court judge have also been added in New Jersey.

NEW JERSEY.

Names of Courts.	No. of Courts.		No. of Judges.	Compensation of Judges.
Supreme	1		9	$82,000
Circuit	21	Held by Supreme court justices, but extra Circuit judges in three counties	3	22,500
Common Pleas	21	One judge in each county	21	69,680
Orphans	21	Held by judges of Common Pleas	...	...
Quarter Sessions ...	21	Held by judges of Common Pleas	...	...
Oyer and Terminer.	21	Held in each county by a justice of Supreme court	...	...
	109		46	$251,180

MASSACHUSETTS.

Names of Courts		No. of Courts.	No. of Judges.	Compensation of Judges.
Supreme		1	7	$60,000
Superior		1	18	126,500
County Probate court,	} Held by same judge	14	} 16	} 44,980
County Insolvency court,		14		
		30	41	$231,480

In each of twelve counties of Massachusetts one judge holds the Probate court and the Insolvent court. In each of the other two counties there are two judges to hold those courts.

It should be stated, however, that the trial docket in Boston is much in arrear.

What have England and her colonies and other states of this Union done towards getting a simple and effective judicial system and procedure? And what have been the practical results? Have they all made a mistake in discarding the machinery which we retain, and have we been wise in refusing to change?

[The plan of the committee of the State Bar Association was adopted by the legislature last winter without discussion, but the legislative action failed for want of the publication required by the constitution. It will be again presented to the legislature this winter and will probably be adopted. It must be again submitted to the next legislature and, if approved, the people must then vote upon it. Meantime our medieval legal system remains. The taxpayer stands the needless expense, the suitor the delay and miscarriage of justice—that is, for the present. But the people have not been reckoned with. Will they, too, adopt the plan without discussion?]

The paragraphs in brackets were written in January, 1902.

CHAPTER III.

THE COURT SYSTEMS OF THE NEW ENGLAND STATES. GETTING INTO THE WRONG COURT.

Let it be said, once for all, that I shall not deal with courts below the grade of County courts, nor with local courts like those peculiar to certain cities. The state systems of county and superior tribunals are to be compared.

Throughout New England the judicial systems of the states are nearly as simple as that of Massachusetts. In each there is one supreme tribunal, appropriately called the "Supreme Court," or "Supreme Judicial Court," which is the court of last resort.

In Connecticut this tribunal is called the "Supreme Court of Errors." It consists of five judges and its jurisdiction is appellate only. There is also, as in Massachusetts, a Superior court, consisting of eight judges (beside these, the justices of the Supreme court are ex-officio judges of the Superior court, but they do not sit in it unless specially assigned to do so). Probate courts, held by single judges, one in each "Probate District," complete the state judicial system. Special local courts are five Courts of Common Pleas in five of the larger counties, and a "District Court" at Waterbury, embracing a number of towns.

In Rhode Island the Supreme court, consisting of seven judges, is divided into an "Appellate Division," held by four of them, and a Common Pleas Division," held in each county by one or more of the judges for the work of trying cases. The only other courts in the state system are the Probate courts, which from very early times in its history have consisted of the town councils. This is still the state system of Probate courts, though the towns are allowed to substitute a Probate court held by a single judge, if they choose to do so.

In the sparsely-settled states of New Hampshire and Maine the judicial system consists in each state of a Supreme court and Probate courts only, except that in Maine Insolvency courts are held by the probate judges, and two or three counties have each a "Superior Court" of narrow jurisdiction.

In Vermont the judicial system is a Supreme court, consisting of seven judges; one Court of Chancery (each judge of the Supreme court is a chancellor); a County court, held in each county by a judge of the Supreme court and two local judges; a Probate court, held by a single judge in each "Probate District."

In making a comparison between the judicial system of New Jersey and those of the great states of New York and Pennsylvania it should be remembered that each of the latter is many times larger in area and population. Thus:

New York; area, 53,719; population, 7,268,012.

Pennsylvania; area, 45,928; population, 6,302,115.

Their respective judicial systems are as follows:

NEW YORK.

Names of Courts.		No. of Courts.	No. of Judges.
Court of Appeals[1]		1	10
Appellate Division	Held by judges of Supreme court..	4	...
Supreme court		1	73
Court of Claims	(For claims by and against the state)	1	...
County court	Held by a single judge in each county	...	...
Surrogate's court	Held by the county judge in each county, except that populous counties have a special judge as Surrogate	...	...

In the county of New York only, there is also a court of "General Sessions" for criminal cases.

---

[1] Ten judges sit now (1902) in the New York Court of Appeals, but two or three of them are justices of the Supreme court designated by the governor to sit (temporarily?) in aid of the judges of the Court of Appeals; 56 N. E. Rep. iii.

PENNSYLVANIA.

Names of Courts.		No. of Courts.	No. of Judges.
Supreme court	(Appellate only, except in a few cases)	1	7
Superior court	(Appellate only)	1	7
Common Pleas	In each county, held by one or more judges according to the population	...	
Oyer and Terminer	In each county, held by judges of Common Pleas	...	
Quarter Sessions.	In each county, held by judges of Common Pleas.	...	
Orphans court.[2]	In each county, held by judges of Common Pleas.	...	...

The curious court system of our state is compounded in part of names and courts still existing in Pennsylvania, and in part of courts which existed years ago in New York. The explanation is historical. New Jersey consisted in early colonial times of two distinct colonies, East Jersey and West Jersey. The latter was settled principally by the stream of Quakers who, coming up the Delaware, founded the towns of Pennsylvania on one side of the river and those of West Jersey on the other. The court systems, like the religious systems and the habits of the people generally, were much the same on both sides of the Delaware. East Jersey, on the other hand, was founded by the colonists who came to the mouth of the Hudson and settled on either bank. New Amsterdam and New York exerted a dominating influence upon the early institutions of East Jersey. When East and West Jersey were consolidated, the first governor appointed over them by the crown of England was also, and at the same time, governor of New York. The consolidated provinces in

---

[2] In the more populous counties there are special judges for the Orphans courts. The state is divided into fifty-six districts, each containing from one to two or three counties. There is a judge (or judges) "learned in the law" for each district, who holds the Court of Common Pleas in the county or counties of his district. In each of the counties of Philadelphia and Allegheny the Court of Common Pleas is separated into several divisions (No. 1, No. 2. etc., each held by a separate set of judges) to meet the volume of business in the great cities of those counties.

establishing their judicial system borrowed from New York the features of a Supreme court, a Court of Chancery and the Common pleas; the Orphans court was borrowed later from Pennsylvania.

In the preceding chapter I insisted upon the practical defects, the failures of justice, that are due entirely to our antiquated judicial system and procedure. I will give two cases in illustration, Homan *v.* Headly, 58 N. J. Law Reports, p. 485, and Smith *v.* Board of Freeholders, 48 N. J. Equity Reports, p. 627. Reduced to the simplest terms the cases were as follows: In the first, the parties disputed which one of them was entitled to a cow and some other articles that need not be mentioned. A creditor had seized the beast for debt, supposing it to belong to his debtor. But the debtor's wife claimed it as her own, alleging that her husband had lawfully sold it to her before the seizure. The creditor and the woman went to law about it, and the simple controversy was whether the debtor had, in good faith, lawfully transferred the ownership of the cow to his wife. The Circuit court, after trial, decided the question in favor of the wife on the merits. But the Supreme court reversed the judgment on the ground that neither it nor the Circuit court had power to consider the merits of the controversy. Such a transaction could be inquired into by the Court of Chancery only. So the parties were turned out of court, having got just as far towards a settlement of their dispute as they were when they began it, and were left to bring a new suit in the Court of Chancery, if the things in dispute—a hog and a carpet were also involved in the quarrel—were worth it. The suit had lasted one year and three months when the Supreme court decided this point. The counsel for the wife informs me that she afterwards regained her property by bringing another suit in the Court of Chancery for some of the articles, and by going through a second trial of the original action in the Circuit court for the remainder. The time consumed in the total litigation was two years and three months.

In the second case, Joseph, a tax collector, deposited public money belonging to a Board of Freeholders in a bank in his own name as "Collector." When he went out of office he refused to pay over the money, or to order it paid over to the Board, and the latter thereupon sued the bank in the Court of Chancery for the amount on deposit, making Joseph a defendant also that he might make a defense, if he had any. He made none, except to insist that the suit was brought in the wrong court. This point the court decided in favor of the Board, and, as it was admitted on all sides that the money belonged to the Board, judgment was given in its favor. But the Court of Appeals reversed the judgment and commanded that the suit be dismissed on the sole ground that it had been brought in the wrong court. In delivering this decision, the judge who spoke for the Court of Appeals said (p. 637): "I have reached this conclusion with great reluctance. Upon the admitted facts, the moneys of the public are withheld from the municipal corporation charged with its control, by a private corporation, without any apparent excuse. Whether it" (the bank) "may justify its course or not might be decided in this case. * * * But the line of division between legal and equitable remedies is fixed in this state by a long course of precedents and even legislative authority is forbidden to intermingle these remedies by the constitutional prohibition against interference with the ancient jurisdiction of the courts."

The time consumed in this litigation was one year and two months. The amount of the claim was over $18,000.[3]

On the sort of miscarriage of justice which is illustrated by these two cases our lawyers are wont to make three comments: (1) "It doesn't happen often." I shall give, in the next chapter, some idea of how often it does happen. (2) "It is inherent in the nature of 'legal and equitable remedies' and cannot be helped." As a matter of fact, it is helped and cannot occur in most of the states of this Union. (3) "It is inseparable from the administration of law and equity by distinct courts, that is, by courts of law and by courts of chancery." But law and equity are administered by distinct courts in Ontario and in England; yet had the two cases arisen in either of those two countries the miscarriage of justice would not have occurred. The court which first took the case would have been authorized to decide it upon the merits.[4]

---

[3] I obtained the dates, from which the length of litigation in each case was determined, from the records and from counsel employed in the first case.

[4] By section 24 of the English Judicature Act (1873) the Superior law courts and courts of equity (they were all merged into "one Supreme Court of Judicature," acting in separate "Divisions") were commanded to administer in every cause both law and equity or either, as might be necessary, in order to end the controversy "finally and completely" and to avoid "all multiplicity of legal proceedings." The same provision has been adopted in Ontario, ("Holmsted and Langton's Judicature Act; Toronto, 1890") and in most of England's self-governing colonies.

CHAPTER IV.

DOUBLE LITIGATION. THE JUDICIAL SYSTEMS OF OTHER STATES.

The last chapter gave two cases illustrating that vice in our system of procedure which makes it necessary for the judges to dismiss suitors from court, after a year or more of litigation, without settlement of their controversies; the dismissal being put upon the sole ground that the suit should have been brought in this court instead of that. In each case the court which rendered the judgment below was of high judicial rank, empowered to determine suits involving values without limit; in each case the judgment below settled the controversy upon the merits and was reversed, upon appeal, regardless of the merits; the parties being let loose to start fresh litigation upon each other.

There is another class of cases, in which suitors are compelled to conduct two lawsuits to settle one controversy. One example of this is a case in which the defendant has a just and lawful defense, but the court in which it is offered, having no power to consider it, gives judgment against him. He can get relief only by bringing another suit in a second court to undo the mischief wrought by the first. A case in illustration is Ruckelshaus *v.* Oehme, reported in 48 N. J. Equity Reports, page 436. There the parties disputed whether a tenant, named John, after having paid his rent for his store for a given period of time, could be compelled to pay it again for the same period. He had made the payment to the real owners, as he supposed, but afterwards one Mary succeeded in proving her title to the store as against the person who had previously been in possession of it and who had rented it to John. Mary then sued John in the Circuit court for the rents which he had already paid, and he pleaded in defense that, knowing nothing of her title, he had paid the money in good faith to the representatives of the person from whom he had hired the place; that Mary stood silent without making objection or giving notice of her rights, although she knew that he was making the payment, and that these circumstances, with others which he offered to prove, estopped her in her demand that he pay it again. But the Circuit court decided that such a defense availed nothing there, and a verdict was accordingly entered in favor of the plaintiff for the amount of the rents. Thereupon John sued Mary in the Court of Chancery, setting up these same circumstances and asking that Mary be forbidden to make use of the verdict which the Circuit court had just entered in her favor. This the Court of Chancery did, after a considerable litigation, upon the ground that John's defense was just and lawful but that the Circuit court had no power to consider it. John appealed and the Court of Appeals affirmed the Chancellor's decree. (49 N. J. Equity, p. 340.)

Another example of double lawsuits to settle single controversies is where a defendant makes an unlawful defense which the court is compelled by law to allow. In such case the plaintiff must bring another suit in a second court to prevent the first from depriving him of his lawful rights. The case of Clark *v.* Augustine, 62 N. J. Equity, p. 689, is an illustration of this paradox. The case was decided recently in our Court of Chancery. A son had sued the executors of his father's estate in the Supreme court for an alleged debt of $5,200. The executors set up in defense a plea that the claim was barred by lapse of time. In point of fact the plaintiff had attempted to sue within the limited period, but the executors resided out of the state, and one of them had given him some misleading information whereby service upon them of the process necessary to start the action was delayed till the period had slipped by. Now, in such circumstances, our law forbade to the executors the defense which they had set up. But the Supreme court was powerless to prevent them. It must have received the plea and given judgment upholding the unlawful defense against the plaintiff had he not betaken himself to the Court of Chancery. Upon beginning a second suit there, the latter court made an order compelling the executors to withdraw the plea they had entered in the Supreme court unless they could explain their apparently unjust conduct.

How often do such delays of justice occur? It is impossible to answer this question with any degree of precision because far the greater number of cases tried do not appear in the reports. But the reports furnish some clue. I have looked through the indices of the ten volumes of Equity Reports numbered 50 to 59, inclusive. They cover a period of about eight years. I find reported in them thirty-eight cases in which either the question of dismissing the suit as being in the wrong court was considered in the written opinion, or two suits in different courts were instituted or made necessary in order to settle one controversy. In eight of these cases the court decided that the parties were in the right court; it dismissed twenty because they were in the wrong court. In four of the cases dismissed for that reason the dismissal was in the Court of Appeals, reversing the decree of the Court of Chancery which had been of opinion that the suit was in the right court. There were four cases in which the complainants asked one court to protect them from the action of another court in which they were then being sued. In six cases begun in the one court and raising several questions, that court either declared that the case must be dismissed unless the parties would bring another suit in a second court to settle part of the questions (the others being retained for settlement in the first court) or actually dismissed the case altogether on the ground that one or more of the questions must be settled in another suit in a second court before beginning a suit in the first court. The same ten volumes contained about seven hundred cases[1] in all reported in the Court of Chancery, not counting a second time the reports of the cases when reviewed in the Court of Appeals, nor the cases in the Prerogative court in which such questions of procedure seldom arise. Now thirty-eight is over five per cent of seven hundred. The summary runs thus:

Total cases in Chancery reported in eight years, about		700
In which justice was delayed or denied as follows:		
As to dismissal because in wrong court—In peril of dismissal, but not dismissed		8
Dismissed on that ground in Court of Chancery	16	
Retained in that court, but reversed and dismissed on that ground in the Court of Appeals	4	20

---

[1] I have not, of course, counted the 700 cases. I counted, however, the cases reported in Chancery in Volumes 50, 53, and 59, which contain respectively 69, 69, and 70 cases; making the average over 69. I believe that the average of those three volumes will hold good for all ten of them.

As to necessity for double lawsuits—Suits in Chancery to prevent another court from proceeding to deprive suitors of their rights   4

Suits in Chancery in which a party was required to bring another suit also in another court   6
                                                                                                              ———
                                                                                                               38

Per cent. of Chancery cases reported in which justice was delayed or denied, or the parties were in danger of that result   5.4

I append a list of the thirty-eight cases in a foot note.[2]

---

[2] Volumes 50 to 59, N. J. Equity, contain the following cases in which it appears in the opinion, either that the suit was dismissed on the objection that there was "an adequate remedy at law," or that that objection was overruled.

	Vol.	Page.	Name of Case	
1.	50	566	Agens *v.* Agens	Dismissed, but merits considered also.
2.	51	308	Pyatt *v.* Lyon	Dismissed by Court Appeals, reversing lower court.
3.	51	337	Beekman *v.* Cottrell	Bill dismissed.
4.	52	813	Union Water Co. *v.* Kean	Dismissed in Court Appeals, reversing court below.
5.	52	275, 282	Bernz *v.* Marcus Sayre Co	Dismissed in Court Appeals, reversing court below.
6.	53	26	Boyden *v.* Bragaw	Dismissed.
7.	53	46	Worthington *v.* Moon	Dismissed.
8.	53	101	Barr *v.* Essex Trades' Council	Objection overruled.
9.	53	15	O'Connor *v.* Tyrrul	Overruled.
10.	53	306	Bradbury *v.* Mutual Assn	Overruled.
11.	53	322	Jackson *v.* Newark	Demurrer sustained.
12.	53	573	Barkalow *v.* Totten	Dismissed.
13.	53	158	Barber *v.* West Jersey, &c., Co	Dismissed in Court Appeals, reversing court below.
14.	54	136	Bellingham *v.* Palmer	Dismissed.

[3]There, were probably more cases of the same kind in the same volumes; for by chance I found some that were not indexed under any of the subjects in which I searched.

15.	54	435	Princeton Savings Bk. v. Martin...	Dismissed.
16.	55	151	Edwards v. McClave	Demurrer sustained, but merits considered.
17.	55	236	Terhune v. Sibbald	Objection that remedy was in Orphan's court, overruled.
18.	55	240	See v. Heppenheimer	Objection overruled.
19.	55	410	Torrey v. Torrey	Dismissed.
20	55	456	Thiefes v. Mason	Dismissed.
21.	56	463	Gray v. N. Y. & Phila. Traction Co	Objection overruled.
22.	56	615	Coast Co. v. Spring Lake	Objection overruled.
23.	58	122	Jersey, &c., Co. v. Blackwell	Dismissed.
24.	58	210	Fahy v. Fahy	Dismissed.
25.	58	357	Krueger v. Armitage	Dismissed.
26.	59	366, 371	Robertson v. Meyer	Objection overruled.
27.	59	530	Palmer v. Sinnickson	Dismissed. Bill to quiet title.
28.	59	26, 31	St. Patrick's Alliance v. Byrne	Dismissed.

[3] In the same volumes the following cases were reported of suits in equity to stay actions or defenses at law:

	Vol.	Page.	Name of Case	
1.	50	143	Chase v. Chase	Injunction to stay action, dissolved.
2.	52	156	Hackettstown v. Ming	Injunction allowed to prevent a defense at law.
3.	55	175	Pratt v. Boody	Suit at law allowed to proceed as to part of case and accounting in equity ordered as to rest. Reversed, 56 Id. 429, because the suit at law should have been stayed.
4.	58	6	Hoboken Ferry Co. v. Baldwin...	Bill to enforce release in action at law.

In the same volumes suits at law were ordered or made necessary on legal questions while a suit in equity was pending as follows:

[The pending plan to amend the judiciary article of the constitution proposes to continue the procedure that caused the results I have described. When it is presented to the electors of the state for approval or rejection, the lawyers who champion it must prepare themselves to answer questions like these: "In how many cases that are not reported do such miscarriages and delays of justice occur? When people apply to the courts for a settlement of their controversies, is it necessary that in every hundred cases there should be, upon the average, five or six in which the parties must be in peril of suffering, or must actually suffer, a delay or denial of justice on such grounds? If it be necessary, explain why it is that in most of the American states, in England and in most of her self-governing colonies it does not occur." Such questions will surely be asked. How will they be answered?][4]

We must turn to the other branch of our subject, our system of courts. I have chosen for comparison in this chapter the judicial systems of those states which have Courts of Chancery. There are but seven such states in the Union.[5] One of these, Vermont, was dealt with in the last chapter. All the

	Vol.	Page.	Name of Case	
1.	55	141, 147	D., L & W. R R. Co. v. Breckenridge	Injunction as to part of suit, and suit at law ordered as to legal title, S. C., 57 Id. 154.
2.	57	91, 97	Essex County Bank v. Harrison	Bill will be dismissed unless complainant sue at law to settle title.
3.	57	142, 153	Havens v. Seashore Co.	Dismissed. Bill for partition. Legal title must be first settled at law.
4.	58	42	Scott v. Hall	Judgment at law in replevin for chattel. Suit and decree in equity to relieve against it. Mistake in contract in which judgment was foun-ded.
5.	58	406	John v. Hughes	Injunction to restrain removal of signs till title is settled by suit at law.
6.	59	190	McCracken v. Harned.	Decree to acc't, but order to first allow suit at law to establish a set-off.

[4] This paragraph was written in March, 1902.

[5] In the other states the functions of the Court of Chancery are performed by the other courts—"the courts of law." In some of these the procedure in equity cases is a distinct

judges of the Supreme court in that state are chancellors, and each may hold a Court of Chancery. The systems of courts of the other six are as follows:

In Delaware six "state judges" hold all the higher courts. One of them is Chancellor of the state. Another is Chief Justice. The others are "Associate Judges."

DELAWARE.

Names of Courts.		No. of Courts.	No. of Judges.
Supreme	Held by Chancellor, Chief Justice, and Associates	1	6
Chancery	Held by the Chancellor	1	...
Superior	Held by the judges of Supreme court, except the Chancellor	1	73
General Sessions	Held by the judges of Supreme court, except the Chancellor	1	...
Oyer and Terminer	Held by the judges of Supreme court, except the Chancellor	1	...
Orphans court	Held in each county by Chancellor and "resident" judge of county	3	3
Register's court	Held by a "Register of Wills" in each county	3	3

Delaware has an area only about one-fourth as large as that of New Jersey; it is divided into three counties; its population is less than that of Jersey City. It is nearly, but not quite, as extravagant as our state in the kinds of courts that it maintains. Its early history was much the same as that of Pennsylvania, the two colonies having been settled mostly by the same people and having the same governor till 1776.

---

procedure, and in some of them the procedure is the same in cases of equity and in cases of law, except only that, in the former, questions of fact are usually determined by a judge without a jury. More about this in another chapter.

ALABAMA.

Names of Courts.		No. of Courts.	No. of Judges.
Supreme	Appellate only (some exceptions)	1	5
Circuit	Held in each county by one judge. Each Circuit judge has several counties	...	13
Chancery	Held by five chancellors; one in each Chancery Division	...	5
Probate court	Held by a Probate judge in each county	...	...

TENNESSEE.

Names of Courts.		No. of Courts.	No. of Judges.
Supreme	Appellate only	1	5
Chancery Appeals	Appellate only. (Inferior to Supreme court)	1	3
Chancery	Held by several chancellors; one in each Chancery Division of the State	...	...
Circuit	Held by several Circuit judges; each has several counties	...	...
County courts	One in each county	...	...

MISSISSIPPI.

Names of Courts.		No. of Courts.	No. of Judges.
Supreme	Appellate only	1	3
Chancery courts	Held in each county by seven chancellors; one for each of seven districts	7	...
Circuit	Held in each county by one judge; each circuit judge has several counties	...	9

MICHIGAN.

Names of Courts.[6]		No. of Courts.	No. of Judges.
Supreme	Appellate only (some exceptions)	1	5
Chancery	The Circuit courts are made Courts of Chancery. Distinct chancery procedure	...	...
Circuit	Held in each county by one or more judges, according to population. Some judges have each several counties	...	...
Probate courts	Held in each county by a probate judge	...	...

Illinois has no Court of Chancery, but I add its court system because it is the greatest of the Western states. Its area is more than seven times larger than that of New Jersey and its population is much more than twice as large.

ILLINOIS.

Names of Courts.		No. of Courts.	No. of Judges.
Supreme	Appellate only (some exceptions)	1	...
"Appellate" courts (Inferior to Supreme court)	Held by some of the Circuit court judges	4	12
Circuit courts	Held in each county by one judge. Each Circuit judge (generally) has several counties	...	...
County courts	Held by one judge in each county	...	...
Probate courts	Held in each county having over 70,000 population, by a Probate judge	...	...

Cook county (Chicago) has also a "Superior court" and a "Criminal court."

I have now stated a comparison of the system of courts in New Jersey with the systems existing in six New England states, the other three Middle states,

---

[6] An amendment to the constitution of Michigan was recently proposed (Laws of 1899, page 479) to create a court called an "Intermediate court," to hear appeals from the Circuit court and other inferior courts. The amendment was to have been submitted to the people in April, 1899. I find nothing to show whether it was adopted or not. The subsequent volume of laws (1901) does not refer to it.

two Western and three Southern states. It would be tedious to carry further the comparison with American systems. All the rest of those systems are of the simple kind, resembling the systems of the Southern and Western states above mentioned.[7]

The number of different sorts of courts and the population, in millions, for each of the states thus far dealt with make the following showing:

	Population (Millions).	Kinds of Courts.
New Jersey	1.8	9
Delaware	.18	7
New York	7.2	6
Pennsylvania	6.3	6
Connecticut	.9	5
Illinois	4.8	5
Tennessee	2.0	5
Massachusetts	2.8	4
Maine	.69	4
Vermont	.34	4
Alabama	1.8	4
Michigan	2.4	4
Mississippi	1.5	3
Rhode Island	.4	3
New Hampshire	.4	2

---

[7] The statement may be easily verified by referring to Stimson's "American Statute Law" (1886), Vol I, page 113, and particularly to the "Chart" of courts on page 114.

The systems of courts stated in these chapters are taken from the following authorities:

Mass., "Rev. Stat," 1902; Conn., "Gen. Stat," Rev. of 1888; Rhode Island, "Gen. Laws," Rev. of 1896; New Hampshire, "Public Stat.," 1901; Vermont, "Gen. Stat.," 1894; Maine, "Rev. Stat.," 1883; New York, Constitution of 1894, and Chase's "Code of Civil Procedure," 1901; Penna., Constitution of 1873 and Brightley's Purdon's Dig., 1895; Del., "Rev. Code," 1893, and Constitution of 1897; Alabama, "Code," 1897; Tenn., "Code of 1896; Miss., "Annotated Code" 1892; Michigan, "Compiled Laws" of 1897; Ill., "Rev. Stat.," 1898 (Hurd).

In each case I examined the indices of the volumes of the statutes from the date of the General Laws to the last published volume of statutes, in search of recent changes.

CHAPTER V.

LAW AND EQUITY.

If an inquisitive foreigner should ask a lawyer of this state why the Circuit court or the Supreme court could not settle the controversy of the man and the woman about the cow, or why the Court of Chancery could not settle the dispute of the board of freeholders with their tax collector and their bank about the money which was admitted by all to be in the bank and to belong to the board (*see* page 19), or why the Supreme court was legally bound to uphold the defense made by the executors contrary to the law of the land (*see* page 22), the lawyer would explain that the Circuit and Supreme courts were "courts of law" and could deal only with cases of "law," while the Court of Chancery was a "court of equity" whose jurisdiction was limited to cases of "equity." If the foreigner pressed his questions further, he would be likely to find that the word "equity" as here used, in contradistinction to the word "law," is a misleading misnomer.[1] He would learn that the people of this state have inherited and developed a large body of juridical rules which define the rights of individuals to their respective liberties and properties; that this body of rules has been the product of a growth of many centuries, dating back far into medieval times, and growing now at a yet more rapid pace than ever before; that by accidents[2] in the legal and political history of England, peculiar to that one among all the peoples of Europe, this body of rules had become divided, long before colonial times, into two classes separated by an arbitrary line incapable of definition in general terms, and administered by separate classes of courts; that one class of these rules had obtained by usage the specific name of "law," while the other had obtained the name of "equity," because in its origin, many centuries ago when English jurisprudence was still in a state of flux, the officer deputed by the king to administer that part of the king's justice was bound by no very definite rules, but dispensed it much according

---

[1] Pomeroy, "Equity Jurisprudence," § 47.
[2] Ibid., § 15 et seq.

to his own notion of fairness in the particular circumstances of each case.³ This officer was the king's chancellor, and till the time of Henry VIII (sixteenth century) he was usually not a lawyer but an ecclesiastic. By force of tradition, by precedents repeated through many generations, and by the requirements of advancing civilization in which men desire their rights to be governed by definite rules, the incalculable sense of equity of the chancellor gradually gave place to the body of fixed juridical rules⁴ which now constitute what is technically called "equity" in the system of law of England and of her progeny. It is, in the main, supplementary to, but sometimes it is contradictory to the other class of rules technically called "law," which are administered in the other courts. The latter are therefore called specifically "courts of law." The net sum of the rules of both classes is the law of the land⁵ and the measure of the legal rights of the citizen. When, as often happens, a rule of law and a rule of equity conflict, the rule of equity prevails; that is to say, the parties are entitled to have their rights determined by the rule of equity. But for that purpose they must go into a court of equity, for the court of law enforces the rule of law only. A husband cannot convey property to his wife; that is the rule of law. So the wife who claimed the cow by sale from her husband failed in the Circuit court. A wife will be protected in the enjoyment of her property whether she get it from her husband or from a stranger; that is the rule of equity. So the wife recovered her cow in the court of equity. The only remedy for the violation of a contract is a judgment for damages in money; that is the legal rule. In certain circumstances persons may be compelled by decree of court to perform their contracts specifically, or even to refrain from violating them; that is the rule of equity. In its origin, and ever since, the function of the court of equity has been supplementary (or contradictory) to that of the courts of law. It was because no sufficient remedy was found for the given case in the list of remedies which the latter courts

---

[3] Ibid., §§ 49, 57, Pomeroy "Code Remedies," § 22.
[4] 1 Pomeroy, "Equity Juris.," §§ 49, 58.
[5] Ibid., § 117. I use the phrase "law of the land" in its popular sense, as signifying those juridical rules in force within the state which define the ultimate rights of the individual in any case within it. If this article dealt with the nature of law, it would be necessary to distinguish between rules and principles. But here the former term is intended to include the latter.

permitted that recourse was had to the king's extraordinary powers of justice. It became a maxim, therefore, that the court of equity had no jurisdiction if there was an adequate remedy at law. No one can give a definition that will suffice to distinguish the field of equity from that of law, because the former did not arise from a great principle of jurisprudence, branching in course of natural growth out of the trunk of the body of the law and giving rise to a connected system of equitable rules like the limbs, boughs, and leaves of a tree. English equity arose rather out of certain accidental classes of cases in which successful application was made to the king's special powers of justice in hard circumstances for relief from the harsh rule of law, somewhat as relief is given now, in the discretion of the pardoning power from the rule and sentence of the law.[6] Now, however, the court of equity is as strictly bound by rule and precedent as the court of law, though the nature of the cases that belong to the jurisdiction of the former allows a wider range for the use of judicial discretion in applying these rules to the circumstances of the case.

With the rise of the different courts there arose also different procedures in law and in equity cases. These differences of procedure were many and great, but the most radical were in the methods of investigating and deciding the questions of fact. In the courts of law this was done by the jury trial, in the Court of Chancery the chancellor or his deputy decided the facts upon the written affidavits of the witnesses, who were not usually examined in court. Thus was developed in the law of the land a dual system of juridical rules and a corresponding dual system of procedure. But, as the sequel will show, the dual procedure is no necessary consequence of the dual system of juridical rules. It is quite possible to administer law and equity by a single system of procedure with a difference in one feature only, namely, the jury trial in law cases. And that difference in method of trial, even now, is optional with the parties.

---

[6] For the origin of English Equity, consult also 2 Stubb's "Constitutional History England," p. 281. For the resort to the King's extraordinary powers of justice, see Sir F. Pollock's article, "The King's Justice in the Early Middle Ages," 12 Harv. L. R. 227. A comparison of the Roman and the English doctrine of Equity may be found in Pomeroy, Section 1; in Maine, "Ancient Law," Chap. III; in Bryce, "Studies in Hist. and Jurisprudence," (Am. Edition) p. 695. For the piecemeal, accidental fashion in which the subjects of equity jurisdiction originated, see Pomeroy, §§ 51, 54, 118.

The twofold division of juridical rules and of judicial procedure was carried by the colonists from England to America. The dual system of rules has become thoroughly established in the jurisprudence of the American people, except in Louisiana,[7] and doubtless it represents fairly well, upon the whole, the social sense of justice of the people who have developed it. But the impassable barrier between the distinct jurisdictions of law and equity, has caused gratuitous mischief wherever it has prevailed. It is, of course, impossible that a busy, practical and progressive people should forever submit in their own courts to such childish obstructions to suitors in the settlement of their controversies as were illustrated in the last two chapters. Accordingly, a chief feature in the judicial history of England and America for the last half century has been a long series of attempts to cure those defects. Before describing these it should be explained that the office of a chancellor or Court of Chancery found permanent footing in but few of the states. In the others, the same judges who have jurisdiction to administer the rules of law have jurisdiction also to administer those of equity, but (with many exceptions) by the distinct equity procedure that prevailed in England, modified to fit the novel conditions of the New World. And a mistake of the suitor in choosing between the two jurisdictions and procedures resulted in a dismissal of his suit; the theory being that the judge was acting as a different court when he exercised a different jurisdiction, and that his power to administer justice in a given case was limited by the procedure of the court selected for that case.

The series of attempts to abolish these abuses may be divided into three classes.

1. In a piecemeal fashion, fragments of the powers of courts of equity have been, from time to time, conferred upon courts of law, by statute. Any lawyer will easily recall such instances as discovery, supplementary proceedings, and the like, which have been authorized in this state for many years. In England, nearly fifty years ago, and in some states since (but not in New Jersey) defenses that were formerly cognizable only in a court of equity were, by statute, made

---

[7] Louisiana's system of law is founded upon the French and Spanish Civil Law. The term "Equity" in that state, "is used in the meaning given to it by modern civilians as the power to decide according to natural justice in cases where the positive law is silent." Pomeroy, "Equity Jurisp.," § 345, Note.

available in courts of law.⁸ In some states statutory authority was given to transfer a cause in its pending stage from one court to another instead of dismissing it; in other states statutes directed that a cause might be "amended" from an action at law into a suit in equity, or conversely, by writing out, with the sanction of the judge, a new set of papers suitable to the change in procedure. Massachusetts, Maine, Maryland, Tennessee, and Mississippi are among the states that have adopted some or all of these measures.⁹ But all such measures, though they afford relief in many cases, are open to three objections. (1) They deal with special classes or symptoms of the evil and not with the general cause of them all. (2) The objection to the procedure may not be taken till the case is in the court of appeal; then that court must send the case back to be tried over again under the other procedure.¹⁰ (3) None of these measures reaches a case where a plaintiff has both legal and equitable rights; in such case he must still bring two suits, one under each procedure. New Jersey has not attempted even these partial improvements, except in the particular first mentioned above.

2. More than half of the states of the Union have adopted codes of (i.e., statutory regulations designed to provide a new and complete) civil procedure. An expressed object of the first of these, the "Field Code," adopted in New York in 1848, was to abolish "the distinction between actions at law and suits in equity and the forms of all such actions and suits," and to provide for a single form of action for the redress of private rights to be called "a civil

---

⁸ Equitable defenses in common-law courts were allowed in England in 1854 see *infra*, chap. XIV, and Pomeroy, "Code Remedies," § 89. They have been allowed in Massachusetts and, I believe, in some other states.

⁹ See the next chapter. Two suits to settle one controversy, are still in use in Mississippi, to the apparent chagrin of at least one of the judges of the Supreme court, who says, "unfortunately, with us the distinctions between law and equity have not been abolished." Home Building Association *v.* Leonard, 77 Miss. 39. One might venture to suggest to the learned judge that the distinctions between law and equity cannot be abolished without a consolidation and codification of the whole body of substantive law. But the distinction between the respective *procedures* at law and in equity may be abolished. They have been abolished (except in the single feature of the jury trial) in most English-speaking communities. Cf. Pomeroy, "Equity Juris.," § 354; "Remedies," §§ 23, 36, 59, 68, 70.

¹⁰ MacRea *v.* Locke, 114 Mass. 96.

action."[11] Twenty-six states[12] have adopted codes of procedure, all modeled upon the plan of the first New York code, and, although many do not purport in express terms to abolish the distinction between legal and equitable forms of action, all except two are alike in expressly establishing the single form of action for the redress of private rights.[13] The abolition of the distinction between the two old forms is, therefore, "a plain and necessary inference from the terms which are expressed in all the codes," although in some "code states" the courts have contrived in certain cases to partly escape that conclusion. Some of the codes failed of complete reform in respect of the particular abuses now under consideration, chiefly because the conservative instinct of Bench and Bar in some of the states first adopting the reform was adverse to it. It was forced upon an unwilling profession by a minority of lawyers supported by a predominating but divided public opinion.[14] The codes did not expressly require that all legal and equitable rights and remedies applicable to the case should be administered in one and the same action, though that intent was clear enough in the spirit and purpose of the enactment. This circumstance, together with the constitutional guarantee of jury trial in all "cases of law," furnished hostile judges with a ground for building up an actual, though not a nominal, distinction between legal and equitable actions going much farther than the mere preservation of jury trial in appropriate cases.[15] A new generation of lawyers and judges has since arisen who attempt to give effect to the reform by more reasonable interpretation of the codes,[16] but the narrow

---

[11] "Howard's Code" (N. Y.) 1858-9, preamble and Sec. 69; Pomeroy "Code Remedies," §§ 28, 34.

[12] Hepburn "Development Code Pleading" (Cincinnati, 1897), § 14. He includes Connecticut, but I exclude it because its system is, like the English system, a distinct advance on that of the American codes. although it is quite true that they are all merely modifications of the principles established in the Field Code of 1848 (Pomeroy Eq. Jur., § 242), which, of course had its historical ancestors. See "Comparative Law," by William Wirt Howe, 22 Am. Bar Association Rep. 572.

[13] Hepburn, Ibid., § 123.

[14] Hepburn, Ibid., §§ 16, 81, 83; Pomeroy Code Rem., § 66.

[15] Reubens v. Joel, 13 N. Y. 488 (decided in 1856), and Pomeroy's comments thereon "Code Remedies," § 66, "We should have gained more than we could have lost had the decisions of the first ten years (construing the codes) never been reported." Prof. Bliss on the "Reformed Procedure," 2 Southern L. R. (1876) 399 (N. S.).

[16] Pomeroy, "Code Remedies," §§ 35, 67.

construction of the earlier days gave a fatal set to the current of judicial decisions in some states upon the point here in question. It sometimes happens even now, in New York, that a long litigated case, in which the evidence and the merits have been fully tried, may be dismissed because the plaintiff made the mistake of stating a case at law in his complaint, when the evidence proved a case in equity.[17] In such event, the court will not permit an amendment of the pleadings; and the plaintiff fails, not for want of jurisdiction in the court, but for want of power to amend the pleadings to agree with the proofs. Yet, making all proper abatement for these shortcomings, the codes made a great advance towards preventing the defeat or delay of a suit on the ground of differences in the methods of enforcing legal and equitable rights. In general terms it may be said that whenever the facts of the plaintiff's case are truthfully stated in his written complaint, or those of the defendant's defense in his written answer, the parties respectively will receive, in one suit, protection for their rights, both legal and equitable, according to the law of the land.[18] Some exceptions to this general statement are to be made, but I do not think that they are many.[19] Had the cases described in the preceding chapters arisen in a "code state" they would not, as I understand the codes, have been dismissed or divided into two lawsuits upon the grounds on which that penalty was in fact inflicted in our own courts.

3. The third class of attempts to effect the reform in question I shall, for convenience, call the British and Connecticut reform. Its distinguishing feature in respect of the present point of inquiry is that it unifies the dual

---

[17] An extreme case of this kind is Gould v. Cayuga Bank, 86 N. Y. 83. Judge Gaynor of the N. Y. Supreme Court reviews the New York cases and applies the same hard rule in very hard circumstances in Dalton v. Vanderveer, 23 Civ Procedure Rep. 443. These cases stand in strong and unfavorable contrast to the enlightened rule and liberal interpretation that prevail in the English and Connecticut courts.

[18] Pomeroy, "Code Remedies," §§ 71, 82, 84, 92 97; Equity Jurisp., § 357, Bliss, Code Pleading, §§ 161, 162. "If the true spirit and intent of the reformed procedure were fully carried out by the courts, I thing that in all the states where it prevails the question whether or not an adequate remedy can be obtained at law would cease to have the slightest importance in the actual decision of a cause." Pomeroy, "Equity Jurisp.," § 358. And see also Pomeroy, "Code Remedies," §§ 72, 73. For a comprehensive statement of the breaking down of the barriers between law and equity procedures caused by the codes, see Equity Jurisp., §§ 84-87.

[19] "Code Remedies," §§ 79, 102, 106; Bliss, "Code Pleading," § 10.

jurisdictions of courts of law and equity, and in express terms requires all the superior courts to administer, in one and the same action, all the legal and equitable rights and remedies to which the parties may be entitled; and provides that if in any case there be any variance between the rules of law and those of equity, in reference to the same matter, the rules of equity shall prevail.[20] Legal and equitable rules remain, for the most part, as before, and in England are administered from distinct benches. There, all equity cases are assigned to equity judges, and law cases to law judges; but each bench has one and the same jurisdiction. No case can fail for want of power in this respect to decide it; and a law case having an incidental equity feature, or an equity case having an incidental law feature, may be decided in one proceeding by the bench to which it is assigned. This reform has now (1905) been tried for thirty

---

[20] The English Judicature Act (1873) establishes a single form of action for legal and equitable cases but retains distinct courts of law and equity, both using the same procedure except the jury trial which, however, may be used, at discretion, by the equity courts. Both have the same jurisdiction. Sec. 24 requires (I condense the language of the act) that in the "High Court," which is composed of law and equity "Divisions," and in the Court of Appeal, law and equity shall be administered according to the following rules: (1) If a plaintiff claim equitable relief the said courts shall give to him the relief a court of equity would have given before this act was passed. (2) If any defendant claims equitable relief or an equitable defense, said courts shall give to him the same relief that a court of equity would have given. * * * (4) Said courts shall take notice of all equitable rights and duties incidentally appearing in the cause. * * * (7) The said courts have power to grant all such remedies whatsoever as any party may be entitled to in respect to every legal or equitable claim properly brought forward in the cause "so that as far as possible all matters so in controversy between the said parties respectively may be completely and finally determined and all multiplicity of legal proceedings concerning any of such matters avoided." Sec. 25 (7) provides that "Generally, in all matters not hereinbefore particularly mentioned in which there is any conflict or variance between the rules of equity and the rules of the common law with reference to the same matter, the rules of equity shall prevail." Upon this act Lord Cairns remarks in Pugh *v.* Heath in the Court of Appeals (7 App. Cases, 237), "The court is not now a Court of Law or a Court of Equity but a court of complete jurisdiction." The acts are held not to abolish the distinction between law and equity. Joseph *v.* Lyons, 15 Q. B. 280.

The Connecticut Practice Act of 1879 establishes (Sec. 1) the single form of action for legal (some exceptions in Sec. 24) and equitable actions, and provides (Sec. 6) that the courts (except some inferior courts) shall "administer legal and equitable rights and apply legal and equitable remedies in favor of either party in one and the same suit" * * *; "provided that wherever there is any variance between the rules of equity and the rules of the common law in reference to the same matter the rules of equity shall prevail."

years in England (it took effect in 1875) and for twenty-six years in Connecticut, yet I cannot find a single reported case in all that time in which a cause has been defeated or much delayed because of a difference between the legal and equitable rights or remedies of the parties. Moreover the reform, although criticised in other respects, has received no criticism in this that has come to my notice. It has been adopted in Ontario, Nova Scotia, British Columbia, and in five of the seven Australasian colonies, as well as in England, Ireland,[21] and Connecticut. Although all the law, equity, and probate divisions of the English courts have the same powers in both classes of cases, yet either may at discretion transfer a cause to the other, and the natural tendency, where there is a great volume of business, to divide labor and to specialize, insures the steady flow of each kind of cases to the appropriate tribunal. In Connecticut and some of the colonies both kinds of cases are determined by the same courts.

The success of this reform has been due to several causes. (1) There had been a great and general advance between 1848 and 1873 in the public demand for improvement in the social machinery of nearly all kinds. (2) The British reform came as the result of a protracted agitation after several prolonged investigations by royal commissioners, and it was founded upon a careful study and report of the whole subject made by eminent judges and lawyers.[22] (3) They had the experience of American courts under the code procedure to draw from. (4) Both the British and the Connecticut reforms had the hearty support of the courts, and the statutes were liberally construed to give effect to their purpose.[23]

---

[21] Hepburn, "Development of Code Pleading," §§ 316 et seq.

[22] Reform of legal procedure was the subject of investigation and of many reports by four or more different royal commissions, on all of which (except possibly one) judges as well as lawyers were appointed. The different reports were made in 1826, 1829, 1830, 1831, 1832, 1833, 1834, 1851, 1853, 1860 (printed in that year), 1852, 1854, 1856, 1869, 1872, 1874. The Judicature Act of 1873 was based upon the report of 1869. The agitation dates from Bentham's time, and from his work.

[23] Brett, M. R., in McGowan v. Middleton, 11 Q. B. D. 468, cites Sec. 24, (7) of the Judicature Act. as to finally settling the controversy in one action, and says: "Every endeavor has been made to carry out this principle and all the judges have tried to bring litigation to an end as speedily as possible." He says that the "fundamental idea of the framers of that act is to

In practice, no difficulty seems to have occurred in preserving the right of trial by jury under the British and Connecticut reform. The constitution of the latter state guarantees the right in cases of "law."[24] That mode of trial is deemed to be waived, however, if it be not demanded before the case is heard. If it should be doubtful whether the case is one that carries the right of jury trial (i.e., whether it be a case of law or of equity) the judge would probably allow the demand for a jury, in order to be on the safe side. In effect, though I have carefully looked, I cannot find a case in Connecticut, since the reform, in which any inconvenience or delay appears to have occurred on this point.

---

be found in that subsection." The cases construing the Judicature Act are collected in Snow's "Annual Practice" (London), issued yearly. Since the Practice Act was passed the Supreme court of Connecticut has said, "It is now an established principle in our law of civil procedure that two suits shall not be brought for the determination of matters in controversy between the same parties, whether relating to legal or equitable rights or to both, when such determination can be had as effectually and properly in one suit." Wells *v.* Rhodes, 59 Conn. 498.

[24] Const., Art. I, Sec. 21.

CHAPTER VI.

HOW TO AVOID DOUBLE LITIGATION IN SINGLE CONTROVERSIES. AMERICAN AND ENGLISH EXPERIENCE.

In the previous chapter was mentioned the experience of the "code states" in attempting to abolish the distinction between legal and equitable actions and procedures.

At least six states, each of which maintains distinct procedures for common-law and equity cases (neither is a "code state"), have made attempts to solve the problem of preserving separate jurisdictions for law and equity, and yet of preventing double litigation in cases which are on the border line between them or which involve both legal and equitable rights. The following references will illustrate their experience.

In Massachusetts, by an act passed in 1865, amendments were allowed, in the Superior court and in the Supreme Judicial court, changing an action at law into a suit in equity, or a suit in equity into an action at law, if necessary to enable the plaintiff to sustain the cause for which it was intended to be brought. By an act passed in 1883, it was provided that no action in those two courts should be defeated on the ground that there is an adequate remedy at law or that the relief sought can only be obtained by a suit in equity; but that such proceeding, whether at law or in equity, should, at any time before final judgment, be amendable at the discretion of the court on such terms as the court should determine. These provisions are now included in the Revised Statutes (1902), p. 1389, § 6; p. 1558, § 52.

An act passed in 1887 (chap. 383) provided that all actions at law or in equity, except replevin, might be begun by bill or petition according to the usual practice in equity, or the bill or petition might be inserted in a writ of summons, and the plaintiff or defendant might, in such case, ask for relief at law or in equity, or both, and the court might give such relief as the nature of the case should require; and that the act should not "extend or limit the power or jurisdiction of the court in proceedings at law or in equity, except as herein expressly provided." (See also Rev. Stat. (1902) p. 1389, § 8.)

The Supreme court, construing this statute, held that "each proceeding under it must be treated either as an action at law or as a suit in equity," and not as a suit in both. (Worthington *v.* Waring (1892), 157 Mass. 421, 429.)

Under the statute of 1865, above mentioned, suits at law or in equity may be amended from one to the other (Loring *v.* Salisbury Mills, 125 Mass. 138), but not on appeal in the Supreme court, because "the appeal does not transfer the case, but only the question of law." (MacRea *v.* Locke, 114 Mass. 96.)

But, notwithstanding these statutes, a demurrer to a bill was allowed, on the grounds that it showed an adequate remedy at law and was multifarious (Workman *v.* Smith (1891), 155 Mass. 92); and two suits may yet be used to settle one controversy, as an action for trespass on lands and a bill to restrain the same defendant from trespassing. (Slater *v.* Gunn (1898), 170 Mass. 509.)

In Maine, by the acts of 1893 and 1895 (Suppl. to Rev. Stat. 1885-1895, p. 423), the Supreme court is authorized to "strike out" the pleadings at law and require the parties to plead in equity in the same cause; or it may "strike out the pleadings in equity and require the parties to plead at law in the same cause, whenever it appears, in the former case, that "the rights of the parties can be better determined and enforced, by a judgment and decree in equity," and, in the latter case, whenever it appears "that the remedy at law is plain, adequate, and complete." By the same acts, equitable defenses are allowed, and when there is "any conflict or variance between the principles of law and those of equity as to the same subject-matter, the rules and principles of equity shall prevail."

But these statutes apparently do not prevent double lawsuits to settle single controversies: for in Harvey *v.* Milk Co. (1898), 92 Me. 115, a non-suit was granted on the ground that the remedy was in equity.

The constitution of Mississippi provides that "All causes that may be brought in the Circuit court, whereof the Chancery court has exclusive jurisdiction, shall be transferred to the Chancery," and also makes similar provision for transfers from the Chancery to the Circuit court, where the latter has exclusive jurisdiction. (Const. 1890, §§ 157, 162.) The constitution (§ 147) forbids the reversal of a judgment or decree "on the ground of want of jurisdiction to render said judgment or decree from any error or mistake as to whether the cause in which it was rendered was of equity or common-law jurisdiction."

A suit in equity having been brought against a sheriff for damages for levying on plaintiff's property under an execution against another, the Chancery court overruled the objection that there was an adequate remedy at law. On appeal, the Supreme court held that "this suit is really an action of trespass;" that the court below had no jurisdiction, but, having assumed it, "we are forbidden to reverse" by the constitution; that the practical effect was that the inferior courts may "virtually abrogate the distinction between courts of common-law and equity jurisdiction." The opinion of the court comments severely upon this absurd result of the contradictory constitutional provisions. (Cazeneuve v. Curell (1893), 70 Miss. 521.)

In Tennessee, concurrent jurisdiction, under some limitations, however, is conferred on the Chancery courts and Circuit courts. (Code 1896, p. 1496, § 6074; p. 1505, § 6109.) There is also given the power to transfer cases from the Circuit to the Chancery court. (§ 6074.) The common-law and equity procedures are distinct. These provisions appear to have accomplished their object. At least, I can find no cases to the contrary.

In Maryland a statute (ch. 229, Laws of 1896) authorizes the transfer of cases between the courts of law and equity.

In New Hampshire, if a question of tort arises in an equity suit, the plaintiff "may file a declaration in trespass" "as an amendment to her bill." (Tasker v. Lord (1886), 64 N. H. 279.) And *e converso*, in an action at law on a covenant, the plaintiff may amend his pleadings by filing a bill to reform the deed. (Winnipiseogee Co. v. Eaton, 64 N. H. 234.) Apparently, this rule has arisen by judicial decision; I cannot find any statute for it.[1]

It is quite plain that, in the first three states, the changes in the law have not completely accomplished their object. In Massachusetts and Maine, law and equity are administered by the same judges sitting in the same courts, but the two jurisdictions and procedures are kept distinct; that is, a judge or court, while exercising law jurisdiction, cannot, in the same case, exercise equity jurisdiction, except in so far as expressly authorized to do so by statute. In Mississippi there are separate courts. Now, the changes in question deal with the procedure, but not with the jurisdiction. They permit an amendment or a

---

[1] I made the notes from which the foregoing references are taken some three years ago; I have not looked since for further changes in the law in those states or for more decisions in interpreting it.

transfer, or both, but they still attempt to keep the jurisdictions, in the main, mutually exclusive. That separation of the jurisdictions is the cause of the evil which the changes in the law were designed to cure. The changes deal, not with the cause, but with its consequences.

Any attempt to maintain the mutually exclusive jurisdictions and yet to authorize, in special circumstances, a bench of one jurisdiction to exercise the powers of the other, tends to raise the question whether the special circumstances are present, and adds to the opportunities to litigate on technical grounds.

The sole object in maintaining the separation of the two jurisdictions is to secure the administration of equity by judges who do that work exclusively. There is a marked advantage in this; for the traditions of the equity bench and the subjects of equity jurisdiction admit a larger play of judicial discretion than obtains in the administration of the common law. It may well be that, in the hands of specialists upon the bench, the development of equity will better attain that just admixture of precision in the statement of the rule and of enlightened judicial discretion in its application which should be an ideal in the development of the law. The spirit of precision in the administration of the common law and the spirit of equitable discretion in the administration of equity react upon each other as they grow, and in the total result, over long periods of time, the whole law may gain more in both directions than would be possible were the judicial work of each branch not done by specialists.

There is no difficulty in maintaining this separation in nine-tenths of the cases brought to trial. For at least that proportion belongs entirely and distinctly to one or the other jurisdiction. There remains a small proportion— say 10 per cent. or less—which involves both legal and equitable rights (e.g., damage for a nuisance or a trespass, and an injunction to restrain it), or in which the facts make a case upon the border line between law and equity, making it doubtful to which jurisdiction it belongs. In New Jersey we impose upon litigants the cost of two lawsuits, one in each jurisdiction, in the first class of cases, and the cost of occasional defeat of a just action, in the second class, in order to maintain the advantage of the separate administration of the two jurisdictions. That cost is the necessary consequence of the principle of mutually exclusive powers in the two benches. But English experience shows that that cost is pure waste; that that advantage can be equally well secured by consolidating the two jurisdictions into one, to be wielded, however, by separate law and equity benches. No one doubts that equity is as well administered there as here; yet they have now had thirty years' trial of the principle of unified jurisdiction. It is plain that the advantages of a separate administration of law and equity cannot be impaired by allowing each bench to deal with an occasional case involving an incidental feature which belongs to the other. Equity will not suffer because the Supreme court, in one case out of ten coming before it, grants an injunction or decides a point of equitable right (subject to appeal), or because a vice-chancellor on rare occasions impanels a jury to assess damages or decides a question of common-law right arising incidentally in an equity case.

CHAPTER VII.

THE ENGLISH SYSTEM OF COURTS AND THEIR JURISDICTION. THE DANGERS FROM DIVIDED JURISDICTIONS.

It is a curious circumstance in social development that many archaic legal forms survive in this New World long after being discarded in the country whence we derived them. Mr. Bryce, in his "American Commonwealth," notes this circumstance: "Prejudices survive on the shores of the Mississippi which Bentham assailed seventy years ago when those shores were inhabited by Indians and beavers; and in Chicago, a place which living men remember as a lonely swamp, special demurrers, replications de injuria, and various elaborate formalities of pleading which were swept away by the English Common Law Procedure Acts of 1850 and 1852 flourish and abound to this day."[1] So, medieval features which England developed centuries ago in her judicial system still flourish in New Jersey (which Mr. Bryce mentions as "a state curiously conservative in some points"[2]), although it is more than a quarter century since the mother country abolished them. No English lawyer under forty-five years of age knows anything, save as history, of such a complicated system of courts as we have, with powers sometimes overlapping, sometimes mutually exclusive of, each other. In the English county court system some of this parceling out of juridical power survives, but from the system of superior courts it has been entirely abolished. The English judges and lawyers who recast their tangled system of ancient courts adopted a principle for their reform, and that principle was unity of jurisdiction. There, as here, the state's power to hear and determine the legal controversies of its citizens had been divided among many courts whose respective authorities were in some cases exclusive and in some concurrent. There had been the same miscarriage or delay in justice in consequence of mistaking the powers of the court; the same congestion of business in one court accompanying comparative leisure in another. There had been the same attempts at

---

[1] Vol. II, Chap. 97, p. 504.
[2] Ibid., p. 501.

piecemeal reform, tried for more than twenty years.³ There had been, at an earlier date, the same apathy in the profession, the same insular indifference to that improvement in the administration of justice which had been effected elsewhere; in short, the same narrow self-satisfaction. But with the growth of the community and its business the conditions became intolerable. Agitation and investigation continued for many years. The result was the carefully studied plan in the report of 1869, made by the judges and lawyers who composed the Judicature Commission. The plan was adopted in the Judicature Act of 1873. The principles and main features of the reform have proved satisfactory in thirty years' experience, although there has been much criticism, and some change, of details.⁴ To carry out the principle of unity of jurisdiction, all the superior courts (except the House of Lords and Privy Council) were consolidated into one Supreme court, in which was vested the aggregate jurisdiction of them all.⁵ The Supreme court was divided into two "permanent divisions," namely, the Court of Appeal and the "High court." The former hears appeals from all the divisions of the High court, but for the purpose of finally determining any cause brought to it by appeal it has all the jurisdiction of those divisions. From its decision an appeal lies to the House of

---

³ Report of English Judicature Commission, 1869, and see the history of the previous attempts at reform in Finlason's "Exposition of Our Judicial System" (London, 1877); and *infra*, Chap. XIV.

⁴ The reforms made by the Judicature Acts have, of course, received criticism in plenty. But all that I have seen have been directed to details. As said by Lord Chief Justice Coleridge, "No man can hope to tell without practical experience what will be the real operation of a new Code of Procedure." See his "Address," 7 N. Y. State Bar Assn. Reports, p. 39. And see *infra*, chap. XIV. I have seen no adverse criticism of the re-organization of the system of courts.

⁵ The appellate courts consolidated were, the "Court of Appeal in Chancery," the "Court of Appeal in Chancery of the County Palatine of Lancaster," "Court of the Lord Warden of the Stannaries," and the Court of Exchequer Chamber. The jurisdiction of these courts was transferred to the new Court of Appeal. The courts of first instance consolidated with the High court were the Court of Queen's Bench, Court of Chancery, Court of Common Pleas, Court of Exchequer, High Court of Admiralty, the Court of Probate, the Court for Divorce and Matrimonial Causes, the London Court of Bankruptcy. Judicature Act, 1873, sec. 3, 18. By that act the Common Pleas and Exchequer were also made Divisions of the High court, but subsequently these Divisions were abolished by Order in Council.

Lords.⁶ The High court was divided into three divisions, namely, the Queen's Bench Division, the Chancery Division, and the Probate, Divorce and Admiralty Division. Each of these divisions has all the powers and jurisdiction of the High court, that is, of all the other divisions of the High court. But law causes are directed to be assigned to the Queen's Bench, equity causes to the Chancery Division, and other causes to their appropriate division, unless there is some reason of convenience or justice to the contrary. If a suitor gets into the wrong division, his case may be transferred to the proper one, or the court in which he begins may hear and decide the cause upon the merits. The High court is the one court of general original jurisdiction for England and Wales. Any civil case may be brought in it.⁷ The state's function of administering justice in civil causes is centred there subject to appeal, and the whole power may be wielded by each division of the court. There is no possibility of conflicting jurisdiction. The suitor who enters it is safe upon that point.

The commissioners who framed this plan wished to extend the same principle of unity of jurisdiction to the inferior county courts, and recommended that they should be made branches of the High court, with unlimited jurisdiction, but that cases in them should be subject to be transferred to the latter on the application of a party or in discretion of the court.⁸ But this recommendation was not adopted.

The sittings *in banc* of the old common law courts were abolished. In place of them are "Divisional Courts." Any two judges of the Queen's Bench may hold a Divisional Court. The judges take turns in holding them. They are intermediate appellate tribunals hearing appeals from certain classes of orders made by single judges, and from judgments of inferior courts. Their decisions are reviewed in the Court of Appeal. In effect, these tribunals correspond to the "Branches" into which our Supreme court divides itself,

---

⁶ The Judicature Act of 1873 made the Court of Appeal the final resort and abolished appeals to the House of Lords. But before the act took effect there came a change in the political control of the administration. Disraeli succeeded Gladstone in 1874, the Judicature Act was suspended till 1875, and the appellate jurisdiction of the House of Lords was restored.

⁷ But if the amount in controversy is £100 or under, the case may be transferred by order of a judge to a county court. "The County Courts Act," 1888, sec. 65.

⁸ Report of Judicature Commission, 1869, p. 13.

when sitting at Trenton, though the class of business they do is quite different.

The County courts as now constituted have civil jurisdiction only. It is both legal and equitable, but generally limited in common-law cases to £50 value, and in equity cases to £500. There are exceptions, however, limiting the jurisdiction yet further in some classes of cases and enlarging it in others.[9] They try civil cases which here would be tried by a justice of the peace or a district court; many cases also that would be tried in our county courts; some that would be tried in our Supreme court or Court of Chancery, and some (admiralty or bankruptcy) that would be tried in our Federal courts. Each county court is held by a single judge (a county court judge), who must be a lawyer. He is paid a salary of £1,500 and traveling expenses. One judge may hold several of these courts in different places. An appeal lies from them to the High court and is heard in one of the "Divisional Courts."

Such is the general system of civil courts. For the Courts of Assize, which are held at stated periods in the different counties, are nothing more, on the civil side, than our Supreme court at circuit. A judge (usually of the Queen's Bench Division) goes into a county three times a year, or oftener, to try causes pending in that division. That is the Court of Assize on the civil side. The same judge sits at the same session by virtue of a special commission, regularly issued, to try indictments for crimes. That is the Court of Assize on the criminal side. His rulings in criminal cases may be reviewed (but only by his leave[10]) on a "case reserved;" that is, a statement of facts showing the legal question in dispute, which is then taken to the "Court of Crown Cases Reserved." This latter court consists of any five judges of the High court, of whom, however, the Lord Chief Justice must be one if he is able to sit.

The Courts of General Quarter Sessions, held in each county by the magistrates (justices of the peace) of the county, for the trial of lesser criminal

---

[9] The "Yearly County Court Practice," 1901, p. 28. The county courts system is statutory and dates from 1846. It has been built up gradually by a number of statutes which were consolidated into the "County Courts Act" of 1888. See "The Yearly County Courts Practice" (London, 1901), in which the act is given in full with notes and cases. The number of County court judges is stated there (p. 6) to be 58.

[10] Writs of error may be taken without leave of the trial judge, but only errors in the record can be reviewed by these and they are seldom used.

cases, complete the general system of courts other than local municipal tribunals.[11] Of these latter there are many; such as the Courts of Chancery of Durham and of Lancaster, the University courts of Oxford and of Cambridge, the Central Criminal court of London, and many borough courts, some of which have a very ancient jurisdiction.[12]

English appeals to the House of Lords lie from the Court of Appeal only. In theory they are heard and decided by the whole House. In fact they are always heard and decided by six or eight "Law Lords" (or a majority of them), consisting of the Lord Chancellor, who is presiding officer of the House, four paid "Lords of Appeal in Ordinary," who are lawyers appointed to sit in the House for this purpose, and such "peers of Parliament" as are holding or have held the office of Chancellor, paid judge of the Judicial Committee of the Privy Council, or judge of one of the Superior courts.[13]

In comparing the judicial system of England with that of New Jersey, we should remember that one of the greatest industrial nations of the world is set against a relatively petty community. Their areas and populations are as follows:

Area.   Pop. (1900).   Pop. Per Sq. Mile.

---

[11] This enumeration of English courts is taken from Mr. Archer M. White's "Outlines of Legal History" (London, 1895), and articles on the respective courts in the "Encyclopedia of the Laws of England." The statements respecting their jurisdiction are founded on the same authorities and also the Judicature Acts and the County Courts Act, 1888, as given in the "Annual Practice," 1901, and the "Yearly County Courts Practice," 1901.

[12] "Inferior Courts," Ency. of Laws of England (1898), Vol. VI, pp. 427, 434. These local inferior courts do but little business in comparison with that done by the county courts. The number of cases brought in them is stated in the English "Judicial Statistics."

[13] Appellate Jurisdiction Act, 1876, secs. 5, 6, 14, 25. Although the Lord Chancellor is the "president" of the High Court (he is not, however, a "permanent judge" of it, Jud. Act, 1875, sec. 3) and *ex officio* a member of the Court of Appeal, yet he seldom sits in either. He sits, however, to hear appeals in the House of Lords. In the volume of reports of cases heard in the House of Lords in the year 1901, I find only eight members, beside the Chancellor, reported as sitting, viz.: the four Lords of Appeal in Ordinary (they are named in the list of the judiciary in "Who's Who," 1901) and four others who were then, I believe, members of the Judicial Committee of the Privy Council. The peers of Parliament who are not lawyers are legally entitled to sit and vote in determining these appeals, though they seldom or never do so now. One such case is mentioned in the "Annual Practice" (1901), Vol. II, p. 479.

New Jersey	8,173	1,883,669	230
England and Wales	58,309	32,091,907	550

Omitting from the list the Privy Council, whose judicial functions are limited to determining appeals from the dependencies of the empire and to some ecclesiastical and prize cases,[14] the general judicial system of England and Wales may be summarized as follows:

Name of Court	Civil Courts Held by	Kinds of Courts	No. of Judges.
HOUSE OF LORDS	Chancellor and four Lords of Appeal and other *ex officio* members	1	5
SUPREME COURT OF JUDICATURE CONSISTING OF[15]			
I. The Court of Appeal.	The Master of the Rolls and five "Lord Justices of Appeal"	1	6
II. The High Court, consisting of			
a. Kings Bench Division	Chief Justice of England and 14 Justices of the High Court	1	15
b. Chancery Division.	Six Justices of the High Court	1	6

---

[14] White, "Outlines Legal History," p. 3; Ency. of Laws of England title "Appeal." Scotland and Ireland have each its own judicial system, distinct from that of England, except that Scotch and Irish appeals are heard in the House of Lords. The Court of Appeal sits in two divisions. One hears equity appeals, the other, appeals in common-law cases. (Since 1902 it has been authorized to sit in three divisions.)

[15] Ibid. The *ex-officio* members of the Court of Appeal are, the Lord Chancellor, the Lord Chief Justice and the President of the Probate Division. White, "Outlines," etc., p. 3. They seldom sit in this Court unless its business is in arrear, when they sit as a third division. Ex-Chancellors may also sit if requested by the Lord Chancellor in office, and if they consent. Judicature Act, 1891.

Name of Court	Civil Courts Held by	Kinds of Courts	No. of Judges.
c. Probate, Divorce and Admiralty Division	Two Justices of the High Court	1	2
			34
County Courts	Held in each county by "County Judges"	1	58
		6	
	Criminal Courts Held by		
"Court for Crown Cases Reserved"	Chief Justice of England and four Justices of High Court	1	
Courts of Assize[16]	Held usually by a justice of High Court in each county	1	
Gen'l Quarter Sessions	Justices of Peace of each county	1	
		9	92

In our general judicial system we have nine kinds of courts, civil and criminal; as many as England has; and of kinds of civil courts alone we have one more. We have forty-six judges (49 now, in 1905), exclusive of justices of the peace and district court judges, to administer justice to 1,883,669 people, or one judge to 40,949 people. England has ninety-two judges (exclusive of local judges) to administer justice to 32,091,907 people, or one judge for 348,828 people. No account is taken here of the work done by local municipal courts in either country. Many of these in England have a larger jurisdiction than is held by corresponding courts here, and in so far do more to relieve the superior courts. On the other hand, the county courts of England do work which is done here by our city district courts and justices of the peace. Judicial statistics are published frequently in England, and it is apparent from even a cursory examination of them that, in proportion to the number of judges, the

---

[16] The Kings Bench has a criminal jurisdiction, but it is very seldom exercised. White. "Outlines," etc., Chap. I.

courts of that country effect a far greater amount of work than ours.[17] No lawyer of this state familiar with the English law reports will doubt that the work is at least equal to that done by our courts in point of quality. Their decisions are constantly cited by our lawyers as high authority. Moreover, the work is performed more promptly. Cases are brought to trial and disposed of much more speedily there than here.[18] In our state, cases can usually be brought to trial or argument without much delay, but the time elapsing between trial and review in the reviewing courts, and between argument and decision, is much longer than it ought to be. A case that is tried in May at circuit must wait, in ordinary course, about six months to be reviewed. If it is taken directly to the Court of Appeals, it must wait about nine months for a hearing. Then usually three months more elapse before the court above will render a decision. In England the review follows within a very short time upon the trial, and the decisions of all the courts are usually announced immediately after the argument. In our Court of Chancery the matter is far worse than in our law courts. At the north end of the state a case ready for trial must, in ordinary course, wait four to six months for its turn. After being tried, although the decision is in many cases rendered immediately, yet it often happens that the parties wait a year or more for the decision. These delays are not due to lack of industry on the part of the able and hard-working judges who fill that bench. To what are they due? How does it happen that in a rich industrial country, having a population eighteen times more numerous than ours, a like system of law can be administered, at least as well as it is administered here, with greater promptness and by relatively fewer courts and judges? It is partly due to differences in conditions beyond the reach of law; to superiority in the average training and experience of judges (all hold office for life) and of counsel. In the superior courts, only barristers can try cases, and they are experts trained specially for the trial and argument of causes. They do no attorney's or solicitor's work. Then, too, the traditions of bench

---

[17] See articles on "Civil Judicial Statistics," Law Mag. Rev., 1898-1899 and 1900-1901. The cases disposed of by the county courts each year number nearly 400,000 most of which are heard by the "registrars," and not by the judges. Of course only a very small proportion of these are litigated. See *infra*, chap XV for the statistics of work done by the English courts.

[18] See *infra*, chap. XV, for the time elapsing in England between issue and trial and hearing on appeal.

and bar admit of a far more peremptory control by the judges over the trial of causes, and therefore a more rapid dispatch of business. But all of these things were true before the passage of the Judicature Acts, yet certainly the dispatch of judicial business in England has been much more rapid since that event.

The calculable expense of litigation is much higher there than here, for judicial salaries and legal costs are greater, and, in the superior courts, two lawyers (a counsel and solicitor) are necessary for each case. But if there be added the incalculable expense to the public and to suitors due to delay and uncertainty in the administration of justice, it may be doubtful whether the cost of justice, relatively to population and number of cases, is greater in England than in New Jersey.

The Province of Ontario, like most of the other self-governing colonies, adopted the reforms of the English Judicature Acts. The provincial system of courts closely resembles that of England. There is a "Supreme Court of Judicature," consisting of two "permanent divisions," one of which is the Court of Appeal, held by five judges; the other is the "High court," consisting of three divisions, viz.: the Kings Bench (three judges), the Chancery (four judges) and the Common Pleas (three judges). In all, there are fifteen judges. The powers and jurisdiction of these courts respectively are substantially the same as those of the English Court of Appeal and High court. An appeal lies from them in certain cases to the Supreme court of Canada, and appeals may also be taken in certain cases to the Privy Council in England. Besides the foregoing, there are courts of assize, county courts, surrogates' courts and other inferior courts. The system of procedure is similar to the English and incomparably superior to ours.[19]

The difference between the judicial systems thus described and ours is not merely a difference in form. It is also a difference in principle, the difference between unity and multiplicity of jurisdiction. A pitfall for suitors lurks in every exclusive division of that power. In a certain measure such divisions are necessary, but in New Jersey they are carried far beyond the requirements of any useful purpose. The case of Collins v. Kellar (58 N. J. Law, p. 429), is an illustration of the danger to suitors that results from the parceling out of jurisdiction between the courts of law. The report of the case shows that John

---

[19] Revised Statutes of Ontario, 1897, chapters 51, 53, 54, 55, 59; Holmsted and Langton's "Judicature Act" (Toronto, 1898); Robertson's "County Courts Act" (Toronto, 1898).

cut down and carried away nine trees which Louis said stood on his (Louis') land. Thereupon Louis sued John for damages in the Circuit court, which had jurisdiction of such controversies. By consent, apparently, the parties, before trial, transferred the cause to the Common Pleas, but did not file a written order of the judge directing the transfer to be made. On the trial in the latter court, John disputed Louis' title to the land, but the judge, deciding that it belonged to Louis, gave judgment for him. Then the Supreme court, without venturing an opinion upon the merits of the controversy, reversed the judgment and set the parties back where they were before the trial, upon the ground that the Common Pleas had no power to decide a dispute of title to land, though the Circuit court had; and also on the further ground that the Pleas had no jurisdiction of the case without an order of transfer—a defect which even the consent of the parties could not cure. The value of the trees (the damages) was found by the Common Pleas court to be $250. The time elapsing between the trial in the Common Pleas and the decision in the Supreme court was about one year and seven months.[20] In the same year in which that case was decided another decision of like import was rendered (Coles *v.* Baptist Church, 59 N. J. Law 311) upon a mechanic's lien claimed by a suitor for work done or material supplied upon a church building. His suit in the Circuit court was transferred to the Common Pleas, where he recovered judgment upon his claim. But the judgment was reversed by the Supreme court upon the ground that the Common Pleas had no jurisdiction over mechanics' lien cases, that power being vested exclusively in the Circuit courts. In England or Ontario such failures or delays of justice would be impossible in the superior courts of original jurisdiction, because all have the same power. If a case be brought in a county court of Ontario over which the court for any reason has not jurisdiction, the suit is transferred in its pending stage to the superior court.[21] In New Jersey it would be dismissed at the cost of the plaintiff, and he would have to begin anew.

---

[20] I obtained from the record those facts stated respecting the case which do not appear in the report.

[21] Robertson's "County Courts Act," p. 78, sec. 24 and 30-34.

CHAPTER VIII.

UNITY AND MULTIPLICITY IN FORMS OF ACTIONS.

The following cases are selected as illustrations of the vice of multiplicity in forms of action.

Guild was appointed, by a judge of the Supreme court, receiver to collect the assets of a debtor against whom a judgment had been rendered. The receiver brought suit in the Court of Chancery against the debtor and others to recover certain property. The suit was begun by an original bill of complaint; it was duly litigated and, when heard, the Court of Chancery, without deciding the merits of the controversy, held that the receiver had no title to sue because the order appointing him to his office had been signed by a judge of the wrong court. Thereupon the receiver got a new order of appointment, signed by the proper judge, and asked leave to continue the suit by filing a supplemental bill in which his new title should be duly set out. The court granted leave, the supplemental bill was filed and the case then submitted for decision. But, after taking time for consideration, the court decided, (1) that a supplemental bill was not the proper form of action, in the circumstances; (2) that as the original suit had been begun before the receiver had got a legal appointment, it must be dismissed and a new suit started, based upon the later appointment. Two years and a half elapsed between the beginning of the first suit and the rendering of this decision. The case is Guild *v*. Meyer, 59 N. J. Equity 390.

McDonald and the City of Newark had a controversy, a few years ago, involving these two questions: First, had the city a right to discharge him from his position as clerk in the treasurer's office without assigning a cause or giving him a hearing, as, in fact, it had done? And, second, if the city had no such right, was it bound to pay him his salary or other compensation for the time it had expelled him, notwithstanding it had put another in his place? In order to settle this controversy he found it advisable to bring three lawsuits, which consumed three years' time, less one month. At the end of that period his third suit was dismissed and the controversy remained unsettled. The first question was decided in his favor, upon the merits, in the first suit which he brought against the city by writ of certiorari. In that he asked the Supreme court to annul the resolution by which the city had discharged him, and the court did so. In its opinion, however, the court seriously discussed, as one of the principal mooted points in the case, the question whether he had chosen the proper form of action. Should it not have been quo warranto? But on this point also he won. The city took the case to the Court of Errors and Appeals; that court dismissed the writ of error, and the plaintiff's right was established (58 N. J. L. 13). This case consumed more than eighteen months. Then McDonald began another suit by writ of mandamus to compel the city to reinstate him in his place. In this he was also successful. That suit was not contested and it lasted only about four months. Next he began another suit by mandamus in the same court to compel the city to pay him his salary for the period during which it had unlawfully debarred him from his place. This suit was litigated. It lasted about seven months. The court decided (1) that, although he had been wrongfully discharged, he could not recover damages for the wrong in that form of action; (2) that he was not entitled to his full salary for the whole period of his expulsion; (3) that he might or might not be entitled, as against the city, to his salary for part of that period, but, if he were so entitled, he could not recover it in that action because, for one reason, he had, in the writ by which he began it, demanded payment of his salary for a longer period than that for which it was due him, if it were due at all. "The prayer for relief in the alternative writ," said the court, "must be in exact conformity with the legal obligation of the defendant;"[1] (4) that judgment be given against him. The case is reported in 55 N. J. Law Reports 267, and 58 N. J. L. 12.

The system of procedure either made it necessary for McDonald to bring three suits in order to settle one controversy, or else permitted him to vex the

---

[1] "So rigid was the necessity of adherence to the prescribed forms, as Gaius informs us, that if, in an action for damage to a vineyard, the plaintiff used the word 'vites,' instead of the general word 'arbores,' employed in the law of the Twelve Tables, he lost his action." Hammond's Institutes of Justinian, Introduction, p 53. Speaking of the plaintiff's pleading in the times of the Plantagenets, Pollock and Maitland say, "It is a formal statement bristling with sacramental words, an omission of which would be fatal." * * * "In a civil action begun by writ, the plaintiff's count must not depart by a hair's-breadth from the writ." 2 Hist'y of English Law, p. 605.

city needlessly with that number of suits for that purpose. By force of the same system the court dismissed the parties with the controversy still unsettled at the end of three years' litigation. Lawyers are too well seasoned to such miscarriages of justice to attach much importance to them. To most practitioners they appear to belong to the class of ills inherent in the nature of the universe, like battle, murder and sudden death. The trial by judge or jury succeeds, in history, the trial by battle, and possibly the sense of insecurity, the element of chance, the possibility of ambuscade in the course of procedure, may be not entirely without a degree of pleasure to the men whose skill in the game is set against each other, at the expense of other people. However that may be, the consequences of these pitfalls to the suitor and to the public make no more impression upon the lawyers and judges who have never had experience of a procedure free from them than did the grotesque failures of justice in the old Chancery procedure of England upon the lawyers of those times, when a suit frequently lasted ten or fifteen years or more, and exhausted in costs the property that gave rise to it. Scenes in which men are bred do not often revolt them. The suitors, Guild and McDonald, had substantive legal rights which the courts recognized; yet, after litigations lasting two to three years, the courts settled, not the controversy, but points of procedure in the controversy, and dismissed the suits. The satire of Swift upon the administration of justice, though nearly two hundred years old, has not yet lost its sting for us.[2] No one imagines that a system of procedure is possible in which no questions of practice can arise, nor that points of procedure may not sometimes involve essential rights, such, for instance, as the right to fair notice of judicial action. The objection to our system is that it so often causes defeat, or great and needless delay, on points of procedure unnecessary for the protection of any essential right.

In each of the two cases the final decision of the court turned upon the choice of a form of action. What is a form of action, and why should a mistake

---

[2] "For instance; in the case already mentioned they (the lawyers and judges) never desire to know what claim or title my adversary has to my cow; but whether the said cow were red or black; her horns long or short; whether the field I graze her in be round or square; whether she was milked at home or abroad, what diseases she is subject to, and the like; after which they, consult precedents, adjourn the cause from time to time, and in ten, twenty or thirty years come to an issue." "Voyage to the Houyhnhnms," Chap. V.

in choosing one among several of them defeat a settlement of the controversy? "Form of action" is a name given to a number of successive acts or steps prescribed by legal rule for the orderly presentment and judicial determination of a legal controversy. These forms, in New Jersey, are numerous and vary much, but the following elements are common to all of them: (1) A formal notice by the plaintiff to the defendant that the former invokes the action of a court in the controversy; this may be in the form of a summons, a warrant of arrest, a writ of subpœna or mandamus, or other document, but, whatever its form, its essential nature and effect is that of a notice to the defendant that the action of the state, through its courts of justice, is invoked to determine the rights in the controversy: (2) formal statements to the court, usually in writing, purporting to state the essential facts of the controversy: (3) investigation by the court of the facts and law of the case as presented by the parties, their witnesses and counsel, *i.e.*, the trial and hearing: (4) the judgment of the court. The differences in the various forms of action are merely differences in the language by which these several acts are expressed, or in the methods by which they are performed. It cannot much concern the suitor in what form of words the notice or the statement of facts is embodied if only both be sufficient and clear. If the trial and hearing be, as the nature of the case may require, by judge and jury, or by judge alone, and if the parties, their witnesses and counsel have full and fair opportunity to prepare their case and to be heard, it cannot concern them much whether the details of the procedure in this respect be of this form or of that. The same thing may be said about the form of the judgment, if it settle finally the disputed facts and the rights of the litigants, and award the appropriate process of the court to enforce those rights. The rights to reasonable notice and to full and fair opportunity to be heard are, indeed, essential rights. No proceeding in which they have been violated in substance should be allowed to stand. A form of action is, of course, necessary to protect those rights, but is it necessary to have a dozen such forms?[3] I do not know how many forms of action exist in New

---

[3] I do not, of course, refer to special statutory remedies. The old forms of action are not abolished by Rules 16-18 of our Supreme court requiring all actions arising *ex contractu* or *ex delicto* (except replevin and ejectment) to be styled respectively "Actions on contract" or "Actions of tort," and permitting joinder of counts. The counts of the declaration must still

Jersey, but among them are the following: (1) Original bill in Chancery; (2) Supplemental bill; (3) Crossbill; (4) Petition; Actions (5), in debt, (6) in covenant, (7) in assumpsit, (8) in case, (9) in trespass, (10) of ejectment, (11) of replevin, (12) of detinue; (13) Certiorari; (14) Mandamus; (15) Quo warranto. There are more, but I do not, at this moment, recall their curious names. Some of these may be brought in one court only; some may be brought in either of several courts; but there is none that may be brought in every court. Generally there is no danger in making the choice of the proper court and remedy. The facts of the case usually mark it clearly for a certain court and a certain form of action. But there remains a proportion of doubtful cases large enough to leave the whole subject beset with uncertainty in the mind of every suitor, and to give to judicial procedure the aspect of a game of chance in which the best that may be said for it is that the odds are greatly in favor of a careful lawyer. The doubtful cases are those of which the facts verge so closely on the lines dividing the jurisdiction of the courts or the forms of action that lawyers, and sometimes judges, can not agree upon which side the case should fall. The consequences of a mistaken choice vary, according to circumstances, from a mere order of amendment involving neither delay nor much expense, to a total defeat of the suit and even to the irreparable loss of the plaintiff's rights.

So far as the different forms of action prescribe different methods of trial (by judge alone or by judge and jury) for different kinds of cases, the difference is justified by a rational purpose. There are cases which are, in their nature, not adapted to jury trial. But why should not any court be empowered to use a jury in any case requiring that method of trial, and in any form of action? For the rest, the distinctions between the different forms of action are, with few exceptions, entirely accidental and arbitrary. They have no relation to a practical and rational purpose. They rest solely on custom, and the custom is bad. I shall not go into the origin of these forms of action. The subject is too large for this paper. It is enough to say that all of the chief distinctions and forms have an historical origin and arose centuries ago out of circumstances that have long ceased to give reason for their existence. They are all means

---

run in the old forms (except the name) and the pleas of general issue to the different counts, must differ. Truax *v.* Penn. R. R., 58 N. J. L. 218. The rules limiting the defenses admissible under the general issue in each of those forms, differ also.

designed to the end of settling legal controversies according to the substantive rights of the parties. As has often happened in the growth of social institutions, the means, in many cases, became ends in themselves; and to preserve them, sometimes even when they were idle and useless forms, the substantive rights which they were designed to protect have been sacrificed.

For remedy of these mischiefs there has been plentiful legislation.

1. The piecemeal efforts which almost always precede systematic reform were used in pretty nearly every community. Statutes were passed in England and in all, or nearly all, our states enlarging the power of courts to amend proceedings, whereby in some cases one form of action may be amended into another.[4] But all these fragmentary attempts to cure the defects gave but partial relief, as the cases cited in these chapters have shown. There still remain in our system of procedure the principle of multiplicity in forms of action and the principle of sacrificing substantive rights in the suit in order to maintain forms not essential to the protection of those rights.

2. The states which have adopted codes of procedure, being slightly more than one-half of those in the Union, attempted to deal with the principle out of which the mischiefs grew. They attempted to substitute unity for multiplicity in forms of action. The first code, which was the model for all others, the New York Code of 1848, abolished "the distinction between actions at law and suits in equity and the forms of all such actions and suits," and enacted that there should thereafter be "but one form of action" for the redress of private wrongs, to be called a "civil action."[5] These enactments have gone far toward effecting their purpose (except perhaps in New York, where the code, in the last thirty years, has, by dint of incessant alteration, fallen into a state of great confusion), but they have not completely effected it. For, in the first place, the old traditions of the Bar and Bench concerning the importance of forms of action powerfully influenced the judges who set the trend of judicial construction upon the codes when questions upon their

---

[4] See McAndrews v. Tippett, 39 N. J. L. 106.

[5] N. Y. Code (1848), § 69; Bliss, Code Pleading. §§ 4, 5. Prof. Pomeroy, referring to the single form of action established by this provision, says: "This principle of unity in all civil judicial procedure, * * * lies at the bottom of the entire system" * * *. Code Remedies, § 44. A special practice, resembling closely that at common law, is maintained under the code in New York, upon the prerogative writs of certiorari, mandamus, etc.

meaning began to arise. It takes time to escape from the influence of inherited conceptions. Certain distinctions in the methods of procedure, which have since been found by experience to be purely distinctions of convenience, were regarded by lawyers of the old school as founded in the nature of primary rights and incapable of abolition. Their hostility to the innovations of the code of procedure led to such narrow interpretations of certain provisions in that law as to defeat, in great measure, its purposes. Judicial construction of late has been much more liberal, but in some of the code states it is impossible, without legislation, to escape from the fetters of the early precedents; moreover, in some instances it is apparent that the fetters of those precedents have been laid, not only upon the volition of the judges, but also upon their reason; so potent is the force of mere tradition. In the second place, the codes, while purporting to abolish all differences in forms of action, laid a foundation on which to rebuild some of them by preserving certain of the old artificial differences out of which the forms of action grew. Thus under an old rule still prevailing in New Jersey, if my neighbor wrongfully take my cow, being at the same time in my debt on his note of hand, I must bring two lawsuits to enforce my rights against him; one for the cow and the other for the debt. The first is an action in tort, the second an action on contract; that is, they are different forms of action. The codes continued the difference so far as to forbid a claim for a tort and a claim upon a contract to be united in one action. Two actions, in such case, must be brought under the code, although all the forms and proceedings in the two are the same.[6] This distinction has probably aided the courts to the singular conclusion that, though a case has been fully and fairly tried on the merits under that procedure and the plaintiff has proved his right to succeed, it must be dismissed if his complaint shows a case of tort when the facts proved at the trial make a case of contract.[7]

---

[6] The codes, with some exceptions, make six or seven classes of actions. Different causes of action may be joined, but only when they belong to the same class. Bliss Code Pleading, § 112. Generally, tort and contract cannot be joined. Id., § 130.

[7] An instance is De Graw *v.* Elmore, 50 N. Y., p l. There an account had been pending between the parties. Defendants, by deceit, induced plaintiff to take some stock and credit the agreed price on the account. He afterward sued for the price alleging the deceit as a cause of

3. The British reform has been more successful in substituting unity for multiplicity in forms of action. The Judicature Act of 1873 established the principle of unity of jurisdiction, as I showed in the last chapter. It also established the principle of unity in the forms of action. It required the court and every judge thereof to give effect in one and the same action to all the legal and equitable rights of every party to the suit, and to grant all such remedies as any party may be entitled to in respect to every legal or equitable claim properly brought forward, "so that, as far as possible, all matters so in controversy between the said parties respectively may be completely and finally determined and all multiplicity of legal proceedings concerning any of such matters avoided."[8] The rules of court made to carry this provision into effect required all actions theretofore commenced in the Superior courts by writ, bill, information or citation to be instituted in the High Court "by a proceeding to be called an action." The rules prescribed in detail one form of action for all kinds of civil suits,[9] except procedure upon prerogative writs.

Had the Guild case arisen in England the proceedings would have been amended as soon as the new order of appointment was procured and the case would have proceeded.[10] Had the McDonald case arisen there he would have stated in one suit the facts showing the whole controversy; the court would have ascertained, and given judgment for, whatever compensation was due to him for his wrongful expulsion, and in the same suit, as I understand the practice, would have made an order commanding the city to restore him to his

---

action and got judgment. The Court of Appeals reversed the judgment, on the ground that he should have sued on the account. But Judge Peckham (now of the Supreme Court, U. S.) dissented vigorously. He said such ruling was going back much more than half a century; that the real controversy having been fairly tried, the pleadings should have been amended, if necessary, to correspond with the proofs. The decision, however, accords with the general rule in code states, Pomeroy Code Remedies, § 558 *et seq.*

[8] Judicature Act (1873), § 24, subsections 6, 7. "Every remedy necessary for doing complete justice in an action in any division of the High Court is provided by" this subsection; Baggally, L. J in Serrao *v.* Noel, 15 Q. B. Div. 559.

[9] Rules Supreme Court, Order I, rule 1. Informations are no longer used in chancery proceedings but they are still used in the Queens Bench Division in some cases. The Judicature Acts did not abolish the old practice in quo warranto or certiorari cases. See Encyclopedia of Laws of England, titles "Quo Warranto," "Certiorari," Mew's Digest, title "Crown Office."

[10] Order XVII, rule 3.

place.[11] I have carefully looked, but have not been able to find any case reported in England since the Judicature Act of 1873 took effect, in which a case, begun in the Superior courts and litigated on the merits, was dismissed because of a mistake as to the form of action, except only certain special cases for which special statutory proceedings had been prescribed. There is the widest latitude in allowing joinder of causes of action. Cases of tort, contract, and for specific recovery (except of land) may be joined in one action, subject to the power of the court to order separate trials of the different cases if justice or convenience require such separation.[12]

The success of the reform is due, I think, to the broad plan and scientific arrangement of procedure made by the statute and rules, and to the enlightened interpretation given to them by the courts. There has been much American experience under the codes to profit by, and it has not been lost upon English judges.

---

[11] The old practice upon alternative and peremptory writs of mandamus still exists in England in cases for which no action or other remedy exists; but in most cases in which we use it here, namely to enforce private rights, the new English practice requires an ordinary action to be brought in which the plaintiff must "claim a mandamus." If he shows himself entitled to it, after trial and hearing, the mandamus issues in the form of an order of court, not a writ. Rules of Court, Order 53; Queen *v.* Lambourn, etc., R. R. Co., 22 Q. B. (1888) pp. 463, 467; Ency. Laws of England, title "Mandamus." A judgment allowing a mandamus, in an action for it, was reversed in the Court of Appeal on the ground that there was another special statutory remedy for the particular wrong complained of. Peebles *v.* Oswaldwistle, etc. (1897), 1 Q. B. 625. But only two months elapsed between the hearing below and the decision on appeal.

[12] "Subject to the following rules of this Order, the plaintiff may unite in the same action several causes of action." But the court may order separate trials. "Annual Practice," Order XVIII. The only limitations are, that actions for land may be joined only with claims for mesne profits, etc.; claims by trustees in bankruptcy cannot be joined with claims in other capacities, and claims against an executor individually must relate to the estate if joined with claims against him as executor.

CHAPTER IX.

DEFECTS OF PARTIES.

Among the mischiefs clustering in our medieval system of procedure, not the least prolific is that which you may find in the mass of rules determining who must, and who must not, be parties to a lawsuit.[1] From many cases in which parties suffering from a violation of their rights have been subjected to needless delay, or have been turned out of court without consideration of their controversies, I select two for illustration.

Henry and Emil each owned a dog; James owned a cabbage patch. The two beasts got together in the patch and wrought such destruction upon James' crop that he brought a suit against their owners for the damages. The Court of Common Pleas gave a judgment in his favor against the defendants for ten dollars. But the Supreme court reversed the judgment on the sole ground that a joint action against the two owners of the dogs could not be maintained. Each owner was responsible for so much damage only as his dog had committed; therefore, in order to recover full compensation, two suits should have been brought, one against each owner. James, being now set back to the point whence he started in his quest of justice, was free to begin *de novo*, with two lawsuits instead of one, upon his hands, to recover a matter of ten dollars, if he should think it worth while to do so. The case is Nierenberg *v.* Wood, 59 N. J. L. 112.

The Education Board of Newark had a controversy with its architects and contractor arising out of one and the same transaction, namely, the building of a schoolhouse. The board said that the contractor had done his work of construction, and the architects had done theirs of supervision, so ill that damage resulted to the Board, for which it brought a suit in the Supreme court against architects and contractor. That court, however, threw the case out of court upon demurrer, without considering the merits, upon the ground that the architects were responsible for their own misconduct only and the

---

[1] For a collection of these rules see 1 Chitty's Pl., Chap. I; Pomeroy, Code Remedies, §§ 184-193, 273-283; Dicey on "Parties."

contractor alone was liable for his; and that, in order to recover against both, two suits instead of one should have been brought. Nine months elapsed between the beginning of the case and the decision. It is reported as Board of Education *v.* Howard, 65 N. J. L. 75.

A celebrated writer—I think it was Bentham—set in contrast what he called the natural procedure in administering justice and the technical procedure; insisting that much could be learned from the former in regulating the latter. The natural procedure, in the first of the foregoing cases, would have been to inquire into the facts as against both defendants at the same time, because the claim against each of them arose out of the same transaction, and the question of fact was common to both of them; for the damage to the plants was done at one time by the two dogs joining together in one act of destruction. The evidence proving the damage wrought by one animal would probably be much the same as the evidence to prove that done by the other. If the fact were that one did more than the other, then, by the natural method of procedure, upon that fact appearing in evidence, the verdict and judgment would have apportioned the damage in just measure against each defendant, either after one trial, or after separate trials in the one action, as the court might order. This simple and natural procedure is forbidden by our system, but is followed more closely, though not exactly, by the English. Our system, by a hard and fast rule, prohibits the courts of law in such case from giving separate judgments against several defendants. It must give one joint judgment against all of them.[2] The plaintiff may then collect the whole judgment from any one defendant, leaving him to get it from his codefendant as best he may. Hence it follows that in our procedure, defendants, in actions at common law, may generally be sued together, in one action, only when they are jointly liable, each for the whole debt or damage. The same remarks apply to the second case. The duty of the contractor in building the schoolhouse, and that of the architect in supervising his work, were so related that the same facts must be inquired into in ascertaining whether either duty had been violated. Some, but not all, of the facts might be peculiar to either case. If the circumstances were such that separate trials should have been allowed, the court ought to have had

---

[2] As to the consequences of a misjoinder of defendants in common-law actions, and when the action may be discontinued as to those improperly joined, see Pomeroy, Code Remedies, §§ 278, 282, and the provisions of our Practice Act.

the power to order them. The compensation which each defendant ought to have made might differ, and, if so, the verdict and judgment should have apportioned it justly between them according to their respective liabilities. But our system does not permit any of these things to be done in ordinary cases in a court of law. It does, however, permit them to be done in the Court of Chancery. That discordance is characteristic of the system. Separate duties and obligations against several defendants may be enforced in one suit in the latter court and it may render one judgment, either jointly against all for the whole liability, or separately against each defendant for his share of it, according to their respective obligations.

The new English procedure goes much farther than ours in following the natural method. In any action against two or more defendants the court may render judgment against the defendants jointly or separately according to their respective liabilities.[3] It would seem to follow from this that, where the damage arose out of one and the same transaction and the questions of fact were common to the several defendants who caused it, they could all be sued together, although their conduct was such that each was liable only for the damage caused by his own act, and not jointly liable with all the others for the whole damage caused by the acts of all; that is, where the causes of action, as to the defendants, were several and not joint. And this seemed to be the opinion of some of the English judges when the question under the new rules first arose.[4] But more recently a decision of the House of Lords has construed the rule upon the subject to mean that defendants who are separately liable upon separate causes of action cannot be joined in one suit for those causes of action. Yet in the converse case, namely, where several plaintiffs have, against one defendant, separate causes of action arising out of the same transaction

---

[3] Order 16, rule 4, provides "and judgment may be given against such one or more of the defendants as may be found to be liable according to their respective liabilities." See Frankenburg v. Great Horseless Carriage Co. (1900), 1 Q. B. 504.

[4] See remarks by Esher, M. R., in Hannay v. Smurthwaite (1893), 2 Q. B. 412; by Rigby, L. J., in Sadler v. Great Western R. R. (1895), 2 Q. B. 688, and by Lord Shand in the latter case in the House of Lords, *infra*.

and having a common question of fact, they may join in one action against him by the express terms of the English rule.[5]

The following I call natural principles of procedure, for in them there is a rational adaptation of means to rational ends, and they are applicable to all general systems of procedure in civilized states. There is nothing startling in them, for every one is recognized in some one or more of the innumerable forms of proceedings with which our system is chequered.

When a person brings into court a controversy with others over his legal rights, justice demands that all those whose rights will be affected by the judgment should have an opportunity to be heard. In order to give them that opportunity some form of notice of the controversy must be given to them in a manner prescribed by law. That is the essence of that proceeding which we call making such persons "parties to the cause." The necessity for such notice results from an essential right—the right to be heard. It is necessary to carefully protect that right, but it is not necessary to defeat the cause or to delay it long in order to do so. If all the parties to the cause have rights involved in the controversy, the court, after hearing them and ascertaining the facts and the

---

[5] The language of the English rules (Ord. 16, 1, 4, 5) is quite broad enough to admit of joining separate causes of action against several defendants, but that intent is not expressly stated. In construing the rule "the cases were in a great state of complication at one time" (Thompson *v.* London (1899), 1 Q. B. 842); but the traditional conception that the separateness or jointness of a "cause of action" is a mysterious force which *per se* should regulate the joinder of defendants, was too strong for the House of Lords. That tribunal, reversing a judgment of a divided Court of Appeal, construed the rule as said above, upon the ground, as stated by Lord Halsbury, that a common-law cause of action "is open to the incidents of a cause of action so as to prevent that which is a separate cause of action being made a joint cause of action"! Sadler *v.* Great Western R. R. Co. (1896), App. Cases, 450; and see the case distinguished in Frankenburg *v.* Great Horseless etc., Co. (1900), 1 Q. B. 512. A similar controversy arose over the rule (Order 16, rule 1) in respect to joining plaintiffs having separate causes of action, and a similarly conservative construction was adopted by the House of Lords (Smurthwaite *v.* Hanney (1894), App. Cases, 494) reversing a decision rendered by a divided court in the Court of Appeal; but that rule was afterwards (in 1896) amended so as to permit such joinder of plaintiffs whenever the causes of action arose out of the same transaction, or series of transactions, and gave rise to any common question of law or fact. 1 Annual Practice (1901), 143. Why not apply the same test to the question whether several defendants may be sued in one action? It would be a much more sensible test than that of the "joint or several" nature of the "cause of action." (1 Annual Practice (1901), 149; Code Remedies, §§ 192, 193, 273, 286, 292).

law, should determine and enforce those rights, awarding to each party, or group of parties, the rights belonging to them respectively. Whether they should be heard together or separately, that is, whether there should be one trial or separate trials, is a question that should rest in the judicial discretion of the court to decide. If a party who has no rights in the controversy has come, or has been brought, into it, the court should dismiss him, charging the legal costs of the intrusion upon the person responsible for it. If one who is not a party has rights in the controversy, the court should enforce the rights of those present so far as may be done without affecting the rights of the absentee, or, if justice require that all the rights should be settled at one time and by one judgment, the court should direct the cause to stand till the absentee be summoned. It often happens that justice and convenience unite in requiring one person to be permitted to represent as a party another who, for sufficient reason, cannot properly be made a party to the cause; as an executor who represents those entitled to the estate. There are also cases in which a person's rights in the controversy are so remote or so purely nominal that he need not be made a party at all. It is a judicial question for the court to decide whether, in given circumstances, a person's rights may be represented and sufficiently protected by another, and also whether one's rights are only nominal so that it would be an idle form to make him a party. For many such cases it is practicable to formulate a fixed rule, as in the case of an executor, but there must always remain a considerable number for which no definite rule can be set; which, therefore, must be decided by judicial discretion in the special circumstances of each case.[6]

But finally (and it is here that our clumsy system suffers most, perhaps, in comparison with the English), if a party has litigated the cause upon the merits and the decision has gone against him, it is not necessary to reverse the judgment, and undo all the work, upon his objection that a third person has not been made a party to the cause. In such case, the court should have authority, if the rights of the absentee are necessarily affected by the judgment,

---

[6] All these are familiar principles in equity, but under our procedure they must be applied, sometimes, in a way to cause great delay upon points which, in the circumstances of the particular case, appear to be very trivial. Compare the opinion below with that on appeal in Tyson v. Applegate, 40 N. J Eq. 305, and note the time (sixteen months) consumed before that question of procedure was decided.

to cause him to be summoned, and the judgment should be affirmed or modified as to him as his rights, upon hearing, might require; the execution of the judgment, as to the others, proceeding or being stayed meantime as might be just. In some rare cases it might be necessary, in order to do justice, to set aside the judgment and retry the case as between all the parties. That point also should be for judicial decision in the special circumstances of the case. If objection for defect of parties be made at the beginning of the defense, it should be decided immediately and provision made, if the point be appealable, for an immediate review and a prompt decision, with preference over other business in the appellate court. With an appellate court in constant session and a well-regulated procedure the delay upon such questions should be very slight, as it is, in fact, in England.[7]

But these simple and natural principles, although recognized, are not put into effect in our procedure by any uniform system. Some of them are enforced in one court or in one form of action and denied recognition in all others; some have a partial recognition only in this or in that form of proceeding, or in this or in that court. The reason for this intricacy is obvious enough. The old English procedure which we inherited did not arise as a system. It arose in unconnected parts. The procedure of the local inferior courts, of the common-law courts, of the equity courts, of the ecclesiastical courts, each grew up by itself and was shaped by the history, the purposes and the nature of the courts in which it arose. In the course of centuries the different procedures, without revision upon fundamental principles, were gradually consolidated into the two branches of law and equity (I do not now refer to procedure in the ecclesiastical courts) at present existing here, each branch being again subdivided into a great number of particular proceedings limited strictly by their respective forms. As a consequence of these historical circumstances, our procedure respecting parties consists of a mass of arbitrary and discordant rules, some of them having only a nominal relation to the ends

---

[7] Ord. 16, r. 12, Annual Pract. (1901), 145, 161. Such questions usually go directly to the Court of Appeal (if appealed) from the judge who first decides them, the cause awaiting the decision. The only long delay that has come under my notice was fourteen months in Smurthwaite v. Hannay, *supra*, in which two appeals were taken, viz.: to the Court of Appeal and thence to the House of Lords. Interlocutory orders not involving substantive rights are not usually appealable except by leave. Jud. Act. (1894).

of justice[8] which they were designed to serve, and, in fact, serving often as rocks to wreck the cause instead of beacons to guide it. In each of the two cases cited in this paper the parties were turned out of court (in one case after trial and decision upon the merits), not because any one having rights in the controversy lacked full and fair opportunity to be heard; not because it was impracticable or inconvenient for the court to ascertain and determine in the action the substantive rights and obligations of each party, but because an arbitrary rule of procedure, medieval in origin and designed to serve a purpose long since become useless, compelled the dismissal of the case.

Of the many attempts, fragmentary and systematic, which have been made in the history of Anglo-Saxon law to get rid of these abuses, the English, being the latest, the most carefully studied, and founded in the larger experience, is naturally the best. The Judicature Act of 1873 established the general principle that the courts should give effect to all legal and equitable rights and duties in the controversy of the parties to the cause, "so that, as far as possible, all matters so in controversy between the said parties respectively may be completely and finally determined and all multiplicity of legal proceedings concerning any of such matters avoided." The act directed the court to adopt rules to put this principle into effect. The rules so adopted permit all persons to be plaintiffs in an action, jointly, severally, or in the alternative, when their rights arise out of the same transaction, or series of transactions, and involve any question of law or fact common to them all; and judgment may be given jointly or separately for the plaintiffs, and against the defendants, either jointly or separately, according to their respective rights and liabilities. If, by mistake, the action is begun in the name of the wrong person, or if it is doubtful whether it is begun in the name of the right person, the court may substitute the name of any other person. "All persons may be joined as defendants against whom the right to any relief is alleged to exist whether jointly, severally, or in the alternative," and judgment may be given against one or more of them according to their respective liabilities.[9] If plaintiff is in doubt who of two or more persons is the proper defendant he may join all of them, and judgment

---

[8] Compare the treatment of the subject in relation to the nature of these rules in Dicey on Parties and in Pomeroy on Code Remedies, Part I, Chap. II; and see especially §§ 192, 193, 292.

[9] Order 16, rule 4.

may be given against the one found liable. Trustees may be sued without joining their *cestui que trusts*, subject to the court's discretion. No cause shall be defeated by reason of the misjoinder or nonjoinder of parties,[10] but the court may deal with every matter so far as regards the parties before it, and may add or strike out parties, as justice may require. Adequate provision is made in the rules to enable the court, by order, to prevent the oppressive use of these rules by unnecessarily bringing in persons who have no interest in the controversy, or to compensate with costs such as are brought in, if such compensation ought to be made.[11]

In respect of parties, the superiority of the English procedure over ours may be, for the most part, summarized in the following points: (1) The English follows more closely natural principles; that is, principles in which there is obviously a rational adaptation of means to rational ends. (2) Those objections which are permitted, for defect of parties, must be made and decided (including a decision on appeal, if the point is vital and an appeal is desired) before the case is litigated on the merits, if it is practicable to do so. Provision is made for raising and deciding such questions summarily and reviewing them on appeal promptly and with the least possible delay to the cause. No demurrers are allowed. (3) The rights of the parties before the court may be dealt with finally, so far as can be justly done, without waiting for absentees whom the court may decide ought to be summoned as parties. (4) The objection can never entirely defeat the cause. For if there is a nonjoinder which must be supplied, the cause is adjourned to bring in the party; if there is a misjoinder, the party improperly joined is stricken out; or, if the plaintiff may sue either but not all the defendants, he is put to his election between them and the cause proceeds against the one whom he so elects to sue. I have not been able to find a case, reported since these rules took effect, in which the action has failed by an objection for defect of parties.

The English regulations are, for the most part, founded upon those of the American codes of procedure, but they go farther than the earlier codes, and,

---

[10] Order 16, rule 11 "Misjoinder or nonjoinder of parties cannot now defeat a claim. It is no defense. Annual Practice (1901), 146. "The Court should never dismiss an action for want of parties." Id., 161.

[11] The rules referred to in the text are 1 to 12 under Order 16. There are also others upon the subject of parties.

being made entirely by rules of court, they are much more under the control of the court in the application of them than is possible under statutory codes. Moreover, in this, as in many other respects, the design of the codes has been, in some states, sadly limited by the narrow interpretations of the earlier judicial decisions.[12]

---

[12] Pomeroy, Code Remedies, Part 1, Chap. II, §§ 122. 286, 304. Under the codes in some states an action may still be defeated for misjoinder or nonjoinder. Id., §§ 213, 288, 299, 422.

CHAPTER X.

WHAT REDRESS DEFENDANT MAY HAVE. SET-OFF, RECOUPMENT, COUNTERCLAIM.

It would seem to a plain man having a controversy, or two controversies, with his neighbor, in which each claimed from the other money for debt or damage, that the whole matter might be settled in a court of justice in one lawsuit. And so it is in the present procedure of England and her colonies. In our state, on the contrary, the general rule is that, if the defendant, in a court of law, have a just claim against plaintiff, he must bring a second lawsuit to establish it. The exceptions to this rule are chiefly in those cases which fall within the narrow and technical bounds that limit the fields of set-off and recoupment. How narrow and how technical are these bounds, the two following cases will help you to understand.

James sued two partners for a debt which the firm owed him. But he was himself indebted for a smaller sum to one of them, named Johnson, for which Johnson had his note. This note, the two partners, by a proper plea, set up in James' action and claimed an allowance for it. After the plea was filed, but before trial, the other partner died and the suit proceeded against the survivor, Johnson, alone. In a learned opinion (in which all the precedents cited, except two, were from English reports aged, at that time, from eighty-four to one hundred and thirty-three years) the Supreme court decided (1) that as James owed one partner only, whilst both owed him, the deduction could not have been made had both partners lived through the action; (2) that had the dead partner died before James began his suit the deduction would have been allowed; but (3) that having, in fact, died after beginning it, no allowance could be made.

Johnson must, therefore, pay the firm debt to James in full, and bring another lawsuit to get back what James owed him. There was also a question on the merits, but the court declined to decide that. The case is Johnson *v.* Kaiser, 40 N. J. L. 286.

Wakeman exchanged with Illingsworth some real estate. There was a difference between the agreed prices of the two properties, and the latter gave to Wakeman a bond for $7,000 to secure that difference. Later, Wakeman brought suit on the bond, to which Illingsworth pleaded, in effect, "You deceived me and induced me to make the exchange by false representations as to the money you spent on the property." After trial, the Supreme court decided, (1) that the false representations were of such a kind that they did not render the bond void; (2) that even if Wakeman had practiced legal deceit (which point the court declined to decide) and Illingsworth had suffered damage in consequence, yet the latter could not, in that action, have his damages ascertained and deducted from the debt he owed Wakeman; (3) that, in order to recover such damages, Illingsworth must bring another action against Wakeman. The case is reported as Wakeman *v.* Illingsworth, in 40 N. J. L. 431.

Such are the dangers which beset the defendant when he is permitted to bring forward his lawful rights in a court of law in New Jersey. But if it happen that the lawsuit be brought in the Court of Chancery an entirely different rule of procedure will govern it.[1] In that court a defendant may, generally, set up any claim which he has against the plaintiff and which is directly connected with that of the latter. It is necessary only that his answer state the claim "by way of cross-bill." Hence the question whether a defendant's rights will be protected in the plaintiff's action may depend upon the question whether the action chances to fall to this court or to that.

A twentieth century De Tocqueville, in studying our institutions, might ask a justice of our Supreme court questions like these: "The American being a most practical people, why is it that you so much multiply the legal proceedings? Your courts—is it not their affairs to establish the rights of the suitors who enter them and present their claims? If the plaintiff and defendant have each a claim against the other, why is it necessary to make two lawsuits instead of one? And how is it that in such case one lawsuit is enough in one court, but two lawsuits are necessary in the other court?" The learned justice would reply (if he had informed himself upon the point) that the explanation is found in the notion which our semi-civilized English forefathers conceived some six or eight hundred years ago respecting the nature of a legal action.

---

[1] As to set-off in equity, see Pomeroy on Code Remedies, § 729.

Their primitive idea of an action was that of a single demand for a single act of restitution or of reparation. For a long time the only defense that was allowed was "a flat denial of all that the plaintiff has said." "To defend means to deny."[2] In course of years this rule was so far modified as to permit the defendant to set up the defenses which have come down to us as special pleas at common law, but (except in replevin) centuries passed before the defendant was allowed to assert a legal claim against the plaintiff in the same suit, and then only in the narrow class of cases called set-off; that is, cases in which the plaintiff sues for a debt, being himself indebted to the defendant. The statutes permitting this worked an innovation upon the ancient procedure.[3]

Yet more recently, and within present memory, another innovation has arisen, in this state by statute, elsewhere by judge-made law. It is called recoupment.[4] It applies to a yet narrower class of cases than that of set-off. In the first place, the defendant's claim must arise from the same contract as that on which plaintiff sues. If, for a price, I let my team to my neighbor, at the same time warranting the wagon to be sound, should I afterwards sue for the hire, the defendant may set up against me, in the action, a claim for damages caused to him by defects in the wagon existing when he received it from me. The two adverse claims arise from the same contract. But if my guarantee were not made at the same time, but say afterwards and upon the subsequent consideration that he should haul a certain load for me, then he cannot recoup his damages in my suit. The two claims arise from different contracts. Furthermore, the right to recoup is not allowed in cases of tort. If my horse

---

[2] Pollock & Maitland's Hist. of English Law, p. 607 *et seq*. That work and Bigelow's "History of Procedure in England" trace the development of common law procedure from its origin to the end of the thirteenth century, when it had attained the fully developed framework of which all subsequent changes, to 1873 in England and to the present day in New Jersey, have been mere modifications. There was no place in the system described in the page cited in the first-mentioned work or in Chapters VII to IX of the second, for a claim by the defendant against the plaintiff. And see Pomeroy, Code Rem., § 729.

[3] The English statutes, giving the right of set-off (2 & 8 Geo. II) were passed respectively in 1729 and 1735. Set-off in bankruptcy proceedings had been allowed by the Bankruptcy Act some years previously. 22 Am. & Eng. Ency. L., p. 222.

[4] Recoupment, in this state, is of statutory origin. Price *v.* Reynolds, 39 N. J. L. (10 Vr.) 172. It is said to have been developed in the other states and in England from judicial decisions. Pomeroy, Code Rem., § 731, Am. & Eng. Ency. of Law, title "Set-off."

stray into my neighbor's field and destroy his crop, and he, in driving the animal out, recklessly injure it, two lawsuits will be necessary to settle the simple controversy as to the sums which we must pay to each other respectively for the damage to his crop and the injury to my horse.[5]

In adjusting the conflicting claims of plaintiff and defendant, our courts are still bound in the fetters forged by our forefathers centuries ago, in the days when judges of the law courts presided at battles fought, on their command, by plaintiffs and defendants clad in armor, in order to try the question of the legal rights in controversy.[6]

Englishmen, being more progressive than we in the administration of justice, discarded these medieval handicaps upon their courts over a quarter of a century ago. The Judicature Act (1873) provided that the court should grant to the defendant, if he made due claim thereto, any relief to which he might be entitled if he brought another suit against the plaintiff for it.[7] By force of this law and the rules of court made under it, "a defendant is entitled to set up any counter-claim that is not so incongruous as to be incapable of being tried with the original action." The plaintiff's claim and the defendant's may arise out of entirely different transactions and may be of different natures, yet if they can be conveniently tried together the counterclaim may stand. The one may arise from contract and the other from tort. Where the plaintiff sued for a bill of costs the defendant was allowed to counter-claim for negligence. It is allowed, though the right to it arose after the suit was begun.[8] The court may not only give judgment for the defendant for the balance, if he is entitled to more than the plaintiff, but it "may otherwise adjudge to the defendant such relief as he may be entitled to upon the merits of the case."[9] The purpose of these provisions is to make one litigation under the new procedure take the place of two under the old. Are the two adverse claims capable of trial in one action as well, having regard to justice and the convenience of the court and the parties, as in two? That is the test, and it is a

---

[5] For a short statement of the rules governing set-off and recoupment, see Pomeroy, Code Rem., § 729 *et seq.*

[6] Blackstone's Com., III, p. 339.

[7] Sec. 24, sub-sec. (3).

[8] "Annual Practice" (1901), pp. 289, 290.

[9] Order 21, rule 17.

test of convenience. Had the two cases mentioned above been brought in an English court, the adverse claims of the plaintiff and defendant, in each, would have been determined in the one suit and the controversy finally ended.

The principle which should determine what claims of plaintiff and defendant, respectively, ought to be adjudged in the one suit is not difficult to discover. The people pay their judges and maintain their courts in order to get their legal controversies settled according to their substantive rights. To this end that procedure is best which brings the speediest and cheapest determination of these controversies consistent with due consideration of the law and the facts. Generally the adverse claims of plaintiff and defendant can be tried in one action with as full and exact an inquiry into the facts and with as ample consideration of the law as they could be if each were the subject of a separate action. If necessary (as it seldom would be) the different issues could be separately tried in the one action. As one action upon a given controversy usually costs less than two, the burden of showing that two are necessary should be placed upon him who demands that course, and his application for it should be addressed to the discretion of the court. That is the English practice.[10]

The code procedure of the states which have adopted codes enlarged greatly the right of the defendant to prove his claim against the plaintiff as that right had been limited by the rules of set-off and recoupment. But the codes fall far short of the present English procedure in this regard. Without entering into details, it is, perhaps, enough to say here that the codes in general permit a counterclaim only (1) when the claims of both plaintiff and defendant arise from contracts (they may be different contracts); or (2) when both claims arise from the same transaction or are connected with the same subject-matter.[11] If, under that procedure, one sues and gets judgment against me for carelessly injuring his horse by overdriving, I cannot recover against him, in the same action, a debt which he refuses to pay me. In such case a second lawsuit is necessary.

The experience of the American states under the codes was before the English commission which prepared the carefully studied plan of procedure embodied in the Judicature Act and the rules made pursuant to it.

---

[10] Order 21, rule 15.
[11] Pomeroy, Code Rem., §§ 772, 774 *et seq.*

CHAPTER XI.

SUMMONS, PLEADINGS, DEMURRERS.

Surely it will be admitted that if the state requires suitors, whose controversies are in course of legal procedure, to use verbal forms, those forms should be designed for some purpose, and should have a rational relation to that purpose: for a form subserving no purpose is a mischievous stumbling block in that path of procedure which ought to be made, so far as possible, plain, clear, and straight.

When a plaintiff begins an action, the first step should, of course, be a notice to the defendant that plaintiff has set in motion against him the legal machinery of justice for the vindication of plaintiff's alleged right. The essential element in this step is the notice; and the more specific the information contained in it respecting the parties, the plaintiff's claim, the step which defendant should take to contest it and the consequences of disregarding the notice, the better that step fulfills the purpose for which it is designed. In ordinary actions every civilized state prescribes a form in which such a notice must be given. Following are examples of such a notice in a suit to recover $500, omitting the formal headings and conclusions:

English writ of summons (used in all actions, legal and equitable).
Title of the court and cause.

"To C. D. [the defendant] of ——— in the County of ———. We command you, that within eight days after the service of this writ on you, inclusive of the day of such service, you do cause an appearance to be entered for you in an action at the suit of A. B. [plaintiff]: and take notice that in default of your so doing the plaintiff may proceed therein and judgment may be given in your absence." A note is appended as follows: "The defendant may appear hereto by entering an appearance either personally or by solicitor at the Central Office, Royal Courts of Justice, London." On the writ must be indorsed the true amount of the sum claimed, and such particulars as will acquaint defendant with the nature of the demand.[1] The writ must also be indorsed with the name and address of the plaintiff or his solicitors.

New Jersey writ of summons.—"We command you [the sheriff] to summon C. D. [the defendant] to be and appear before the Supreme court to be held at Trenton on the ―――― day of ――――, 1903, to answer unto A. B. [the plaintiff] in an action upon contract wherein the plaintiff demands one thousand dollars. And have you then and there this writ." The name and address of the plaintiff or his attorney must be indorsed.

New Jersey writ of subpœna.—"We command you, that you appear in manner and form required by law in our Court of Chancery, on the ―――― day of ――――, at Trenton, to answer to a bill of complaint exhibited against you in our said court by A. B., and to do further and receive what our said court shall have considered in that behalf; and this you are not to omit, under the penalty that may fall thereon." The writ of subpœna (but not the writ of summons) has appended the following note: "The defendant is not required to appear at Trenton in person, at the return day, but, if he intends to make a defense it is only necessary for him to answer, plead or demur to the bill within the time required by law."

The form of the English writ precisely fulfills its purpose of a notice. Every detail of which the defendant should be informed at this stage of the suit is exactly imparted. Our writ of summons is a misleading and insufficient notice. It falsifies in respect of defendant's appearance in Trenton, and in respect of the amount of the plaintiff's demand, which is never truly stated, and it is insufficient in that it does not give information respecting the nature of the claim or of the consequences of nonappearance. I have been informed in the office of the clerk of the Supreme court that it is a common occurrence to have visits there from defendants who come to Trenton from a long distance in supposed obedience to these lying summonses. The writ of subpoena does not mislead, but it does not give adequate information as the English writ of summons does. Neither the nature of the action, nor the sum demanded, nor the consequence of nonappearance is mentioned in our writ.

After a defendant is notified in due form of the beginning of a suit against him, the step next usually taken is presenting a formal written statement of the

---

[1] Annual Practice (1901), Order 3, rule 4. For the forms, see Annual Practice, vol. 2, p. 1.

plaintiff's claim. The purposes of written pleadings are: (1) to expedite the cause by sifting the disputed facts in the controversy from those which are not disputed; (2) to show the essential facts alleged by each party with such reasonable fullness and precision as will enable the opposite party to answer or disprove them; (3) to preserve a record of the controversy and of the judgment upon it. In most cases in which the plaintiff or defendant is required, in our system of procedure, to declare or plead specially, our rules of pleading reasonably fulfill the foregoing ends, although with grotesque prolixity; but in a great number of cases the plaintiff declares on common counts only, and in many cases the defendant pleads the general issue only. In such cases neither the declaration nor the plea performs one of the foregoing natural and essential functions of a pleading. A comparison will illustrate this statement. Legal procedure in Connecticut is not governed by a code. Common-law procedure prevails, but is modified by the short Practice Act of 1879 and by the rules of court which were founded, in part on American codes but in a large measure, upon the new English procedure. Here is a declaration in the Connecticut form[2] for goods sold when no price is agreed on, and for a promissory note for money lent. The declaration is prefaced with a copy of the summons.

"First Count.
    "1. On May 1, 1902, the plaintiff sold and delivered to the defendant one hundred barrels of flour at a reasonable price, payable on their delivery.
    "2. The same were reasonably worth $600.
    "3. The defendant has not paid the same.

"Second Count.
    "1. On June 1, 1902, the defendant, by his note of that date, promised to pay the plaintiff $1,000 thirty days after date, for value received.
    "2. The defendant has not paid the same."
    The dates and amounts of money are required to be stated truthfully.

---

[2] Beers' Connecticut Practice Act (1901), p. 25.

In England the "statement of claim" (declaration) would be as follows:[3]

"1. The plaintiff's claim is for the price of goods sold and delivered.
Particulars:

May 1, 1902, 100 barrels of flour $600

"2. The plaintiff's claim is also against the defendant, as maker of a promissory note for $1,000 dated June 1, 1902, payable thirty days after date.
Particulars:

Principal $1,000.00
Interest 65.00
$1,065.00"

In the New Jersey procedure the declaration for the same demands would probably be as follows:

"For that whereas the said defendant on the first day of March, 1903 (or any day before beginning suit), at Jersey City in the county of Hudson aforesaid (though the obligation may have been incurred in some other town and county) was indebted to the plaintiff in twelve hundred dollars (or any sum more than the true sum) for the price and value of goods sold and delivered by the plaintiff to the defendant at his request; and in the sum of two thousand dollars for money lent by the plaintiff to the defendant at his request. And being so indebted the defendant afterward, to wit, on the day and year last aforesaid, in the county aforesaid, in consideration of the premises, respectively promised to pay the said several sums of money respectively to the plaintiff on request. Yet the defendant, though often requested, has disregarded his promises and has not paid any of said money or any part thereof. To the plaintiff's damage thirty-two hundred dollars, and thereupon he brings his, suit," etc.

The declaration would probably contain the other common counts also, as they are all printed together in the form usually employed; but being unnecessary I omit them. It is true that copies of the bill of goods and of the

---

[3] The form is taken from Annual Practice (1901), vol. 2, pp. 50, 51. "Every pleading shall contain, and contain only, a statement in a summary form of the material facts on which the party pleading relies for his claim or defense, as the case may be, but not the evidence by which they are to be proved, and shall, where necessary, be divided into paragraphs numbered consecutively. Dates, sums and numbers shall be expressed in figures and not in words." Order 19, rule 4.

note will probably be attached, but these are not part of the declaration. That document itself is stuffed with falsehoods.

To this useless pleading the defendant will, except in a few unusual cases, reply by a pleading still more useless for any purpose that a pleading is designed to serve. He will plead the general issue, which merely denies that he made the promises stated in the declaration, and that, though he intends to admit them at the trial and show some other defense, for example, that he has performed them by paying the debts. By means of special written demands for the particulars of plaintiff's claim or of defendant's defense, the real facts in controversy may be, at last, evoked, but that result is attained, not by the pleadings, but in spite of them. In practice, these pleadings serve the purpose of concealing the facts which, in theory, they are designed to set forth. It is also true that, in one way or another, knowledge of the real facts is at last attained. That was also true of the old action of ejectment in which a fictitious plaintiff brought an action on a fictitious lease against a fictitious defendant to recover a fictitious term of years.

But if plaintiff sets out, or attempts to set out, in his declaration the real facts of the controversy the question may arise whether, upon those facts, he is entitled to an action against the defendant. If that question arise upon the facts which the plaintiff intends to prove at the trial, it becomes a point of substantive right, the decision of which may finally settle the controversy; and being such, it should be heard and decided with the deliberation due to its importance. But if the question arise, not on the facts as the plaintiff believes them to be, but upon a misstatement of them, which, by a slip, he has allowed to creep into his declaration, it is a sheer abuse to spend any more time upon the business than is necessary to cause the mistake to be corrected. Yet, under our mediæval procedure, precisely the same time is taken to decide the point in the one case as in the other. Here is one of numberless cases in illustration. Henry sold goods to Jeremiah, which, subsequently, the latter refused to accept and pay for. Henry thereupon sued him for damages, and in his declaration averred that the defendant had agreed to accept and pay for the goods at a time and place which the declaration specifically stated. The pleader, however, omitted to say in that document that plaintiff was ready at the agreed time and place to deliver the goods and accept the price. For this reason (and another of no more apparent substance) the declaration was adjudged by the court to be bad on demurrer. The case is Leslie *v.* Carey, 59 N. J. L. 6. Although the point was fatal to the declaration, the defect must have been a mere slip in statement by the pleader, for it appears not to have been noticed in the argument by counsel on either side (page 8), for they contested sundry other points and did not raise this one. Such verbal defects could be remedied in a few minutes with practically no delay to the progress of the cause, by requiring objections to them to be summarily heard and decided on short notice before a single judge armed with power to amend the defective pleading into proper form upon the spot.

In another case the real controversy was whether the defendants were bound to pay a bond they had given to the plaintiff conditioned that one of them should appear before "the then next" Court of Common Pleas, and petition for the benefit of the insolvent laws. The defendant pleaded that they had so appeared and petitioned at "a subsequent" Court of Common Pleas, naming the day and date. On demurrer to the plea, the court decided that "a subsequent" court was not necessarily the "then next court," though there was no attempt to ascertain whether it was so in fact, and gave judgment, with costs, against the defendant as for a bad plea. The case is Hart *v.* Boyle, 60 N. J. L. 320. Over such childish quibbles counsel upon both sides and four justices of the Supreme court spent what time was taken respectively in preparing, arguing and deciding the two cases, and in writing two opinions. The suitors in each case waited four months after the argument ere the court pronounced its decision.

There is no place in the English procedure for this silly waste of time. Demurrers are abolished. A party may raise a point of law in the pleading in which he answers his opponent, and that point will be disposed of at the trial when the whole merits of the case are considered, unless the judge, on application of either party, thinks justice or convenience requires it to be heard before trial.[4] Or either party may move to strike out his adversary's

---

[4] "No demurrer shall be allowed." Order 25, rule 1. "Any party shall be entitled to raise by his pleading any point of law, and any point so raised shall be disposed of by the judge who tries the cause at or after the trial; provided, that by consent of the parties or by order of the court or judge, on the application of either party, the same may be set down for hearing and disposed of at any time before the trial." Order 25, rule 2.

pleading on the ground that it is obviously bad, which motion is summarily decided by the court or a single judge.[5]

Many of the useless delays upon demurrer, are occasioned by a violation of certain ancient, formal, rules of pleading which are now entirely useless. These rules, or most of them, were designed to compel the parties to reach a "single issue," on which the fate of the whole case must depend. The single issue is never compelled now, but the rules of pleading designed to compel it are still enforced, though they have become purposeless. If you do not observe them, your pleading may generally be demurred to, and if your case is in the Supreme court you will, probably, wait from four to seven or eight months before the court decides whether you have violated the aimless rule which it must enforce against you.

---

[5] Order 25, rule 4.

CHAPTER XII.

JUDGMENTS.

Since the times of the Plantagenets, judgments, in common-law actions, have run always in certain fixed forms of words. If the facts in controversy in the action showed a juridical right in one of the litigants which could not be protected or enforced by a judgment in one of those forms, the party was remediless in that court unless a statute could be found which armed the court with the special power necessary to administer justice in such a case. And that is the system of procedure now prevailing in New Jersey. To this day, a court of common law has neither a form of judgment nor the power to prevent my neighbor from repeating his trespasses on my property after it has found him guilty of such a wrong and mulcted him in damages for it. It does not matter just now whether the want of power originated in the want of a form, or whether absence of a form was due, in those early days, to absence of power. Both the power and the form are wanting now in our Supreme court in such a simple case as I have just mentioned. The explanation of this curious maladjustment of our machinery of justice to its work is to be found in the legal conceptions framed by our forefathers in the days of the Crusades. When the foundations of the English system of legal procedure were being laid in the twelfth and thirteenth centuries, the jurisdiction of the royal courts to hear any case was conditioned upon the authority conferred for that particular case by the "original writ" which the plaintiff procured from "the Chancery" as the first step in his procedure.[1] The jurisdiction, moreover, was limited to hearing and deciding the precise point which the writ stated and referred to the court for inquiry and decision. The writs at last fell into certain fixed formulæ out of which grew the "forms of action;" and the judgments naturally fell into correspondingly fixed and simple forms of affirmative or

---

[1] Bigelow, "History Procedure in England," 196; 1 Chitty's Pleadings, p. 95; 1 Poll. Mait. Hist. English Law, p. 194.

negative decision.² If the facts of the case would not fit into one of these forms of action, neither would the corresponding form of judgment fit the facts, and the party could have no relief. It was this narrowness in the play of judicial action in the courts of law that gave rise to the equitable jurisdiction of the chancellor, and, with many modifications, the same narrowness hampers the courts which now do most of the work of litigation in our state.

For example, my neighbor, John, alleges that a testator, of whose estate I am executor and trustee, damaged his (John's) field by repeatedly driving across it, and that I, while administering the business of the estate, have continued the same practice. He forbids further trespassing and demands payment for the damages caused by my testator's acts and by mine also. I reply that he granted to testator the right to drive over the field; that I, as executor and devisee in trust, have succeeded to the right; that the people entitled to the estate insist upon my asserting it; moreover, that when he granted the right of way, as one of the inducements thereto, testator had loaned him a sum of money which he still owes to the estate. John denies the grant, says he paid the debt to testator, and, as we can agree on none of these points, we go to law. Now, if the quarrel were to be determined in a suit brought by John against me in one of the Superior courts of England, or Ireland, or Ontario, or Nova Scotia, or New Zealand, or South Australia, or Victoria,³ the whole controversy and every dispute in it could be finally settled in one lawsuit. After trial of the several issues of fact, in one, or in separate, trials, as the court might think just and convenient, the judgment would find: (1) The balance (if anything) due upon John's debt; (2) Whether or not my testator had, and I have, a right to drive across the field; (3) If no such right existed, then how

---

² "The formula in which the judgment was pronounced, according to the result of the trial, being reduced to writing on the record, acquired in time, from similar causes, the same fixed and unalterable character which distinguished the breve and the pleadings; each form of action given by the breve having an appropriate formula of judgment." 1 Burrill's Practice, p. 16. The fixed forms of all kinds of judgments at common law in civil actions may be found in almost any book on common-law practice; see, for instance, 1 Burrill's Pr., chap. IV. Of course, where a statute directs a law court to afford a particular relief or render a special kind of judgment, it must, and does, modify the ordinary forms so far as is necessary to obey the statute; as, for instance, in Mechanics' Liens cases.

³ The reformed English procedure has been adopted in Ireland and in all of the English colonies mentioned above.

much damage had been inflicted upon John by the trespasses of the testator and of his executor; (4) That the difference between the balance of the debt and the amount of the damages should be paid to the party to whom it was due; (5) That I be forbidden by the injunction of the court from further trespassing.[4] It is true that the court could require separate suits to be brought if it appeared that a practical inconvenience would attend the trial of the different issues in one. But the party asserting such inconvenience must show it to the satisfaction of the court. I have not heard that the smallest difficulty has been found in practice in this method of comprehensive settlement of the whole controversy in the English procedure, and it has stood the test of an experience of thirty years.

But in New Jersey, no court has authority to frame a judgment which could, in one suit, determine and finally settle all of these points in controversy. The decree of the Court of Chancery is flexible enough in form, but the court has no power to award damages. The judgment of a court of law, on the other hand, is among the most inflexible of legal instruments. There is no form known to a common-law court in which a judgment could be framed in one action to settle the rights shown in such a case as the foregoing. If the right of way did not in fact exist, four law suits would be necessary in order to make complete settlement of the controversy according to the substantive rights of the parties, namely: (1) a suit at law by John against me as executor for the trespasses committed by my testator; (2) another suit at law by John against me individually, for the trespasses committed by me, though I had done the acts in the necessary discharge of my duties as executor and trustee, and at the request of the persons entitled to the estate; (3) a suit by him against me in Chancery to restrain me from further trespassing; and (4) a suit at law by me against John to recover the debt due upon the debt.

---

[4] As stated in chap. X, the present English procedure permits a, counterclaim in contract to be set up in a suit by plaintiff for a tort, if the two claims can be conveniently tried together; and the judgment will be framed to give defendant whatever relief he is entitled to by substantive law. Claims by or against an executor or administrator as such may be joined with claims against him personally, provided the personal claims arise with reference to the estate which he represents. Order 18, Rule 5. Since the Judicature Act of 1873, the English courts constantly grant injunctions in actions on common-law rights. The writ of injunction is abolished. All injunctions are in the form of judgments or orders of court. Order 50, rule 11.

Under the artificial rules of our procedure, it would not be possible to simplify the litigation except by leaving some point unsettled. The claim upon the debt and the claim for the trespasses could not be settled in one suit; not because two suits are more convenient than one, but because one claim arises from contract and the other from tort. The claim for trespasses committed by testator and the claim for trespasses committed by his executor, even though both claims must be finally paid from the same estate, could not be settled in one suit; not because of any inconvenience in doing so, but because an artificial rule of law, framed to fit the legal conceptions which Englishmen entertained in the Middle Ages, forbids the uniting, in one action, of a claim against an estate and a personal claim against its executor (a tort committed by the executor is, by a like technical rule, always a personal claim against him). The claim for an injunction could not be included in a suit for any of the other claims; not because of any reason founded in justice or common sense, but because the English judges, in the days of castles, of battle-axes and of bows and arrows, did not conceive the idea of the prevention of an injury as a function of their courts of law, nor frame a form of judgment to give effect to such a function.[5]

---

[5] There appears to have been an exception in actions of waste, in which, at an ancient day, the court of law could forbid further waste. 2 Pollock & Maitland, History of English Law, p. 596.

CHAPTER XIII.

APPELLATE PROCEDURE.

Our appellate procedure is far from simple. Certain classes of cases must be reviewed in this court, other classes in that court, other classes again in another court. Some must be reviewed by this procedure, some by that. A mistake in the choice is visited with the penalty either of a dismissal of the proceeding, or, as often happens, of the loss of the right to the appeal. The circumstances of your case may be upon the border line dividing one class from another; in which event you make your guess before the court, as the Thebans made theirs before the Sphinx, at the risk of destruction. Some judgments of a justice's court must be reviewed by certiorari in the Supreme court, some by appeal in the Common Pleas, and some may be reviewed by either.[1] To review a decision of the surrogate, the suitor must decide whether his case is of the class which must be taken to the Orphans' court or to the Prerogative court.[2] If you wish to review an order of the Orphans' court for want of jurisdiction, you must decide, at your peril, whether to take a certiorari to the Supreme court or an appeal to the Prerogative court.[3] If your case is in the Common Pleas you may be obliged to take a certiorari or, on the other hand, a writ of error, according to the circumstances of the case.[4] If you take one when you should take the other, your case may be dismissed, with costs. The writ of error to review a judgment of the Common Pleas can issue from the Supreme court only; to review a judgment of the Circuit court, it may issue from either the Supreme court or the Court of Errors and Appeals. A decision upon the facts by a judge (a jury having been waived) is final in a

---

[1] Ritter *v.* Kunkle, 39 N. J. L. 259.

[2] Orphans' Court Act, Rev. 1898, sec. 203.

[3] The certiorari was dismissed in Carroll *v.* Baxter, 65 N. J. L. 478, on the ground that when the Orphans' court has jurisdiction, appeal is the only method of review. Contra, when there is no jurisdiction. Potter *v.* Berry, 56 N. J. L. 454.

[4] If it be a judgment on a justices' appeal, certiorari is the appellate proceeding; if the suit originated in the Common Pleas and it had jurisdiction, a writ of error Steamboat Co. *v.* Flanagan, 41 N. J. L. 115; Albert *v.* Hart, 44 id. 366.

court of law; in a court of equity or of probate it is not final but may be reviewed on appeal, unless the appellate procedure be by certiorari, in which event the facts cannot be reviewed.

What is the reason for this labyrinthine intricacy? There is no reason. There is, however, a cause. The determining factor in the question whether you shall take this court or procedure, or that, is (saving a few exceptions) neither the interest of the suitors in a speedy and final adjustment of their rights, nor of the state in limiting the public cost of litigation. The determining factor in each case is, generally, an arbitrary rule caused by piecemeal attempts to graft readjustments suited to the conditions of the Nineteenth century upon three mutually exclusive systems[5] of appellate procedure which arose in England during the Middle Ages in adjustment to the social conditions of those times.

If your case chance to be an appeal to the Prerogative court, the procedure will be exceedingly simple, untechnical and speedy. If, on the other hand, it be a writ of error from the Supreme court or Court of Errors and Appeals, you will find the procedure technical and dangerous. I have never heard of an appeal that miscarried in the Prerogative court from defects in procedure, but in the others I know of a great many. Here are some cases in illustration.

A defendant in the Common Pleas offered to prove a certain defense, but the court overruled it and gave judgment against him. On writ of error the Supreme court said that there was "manifest error" in overruling the defense. That court, however, did not reverse the judgment. On the contrary, it dismissed the writ of error. Not because of any circumstance that bore any, even the most distant, relation to the merits of the case or the rights of the parties, but because (1) only a rule for judgment, instead of the formal judgment, below was among the papers returned with the writ of error; and (2) "a statement of facts made by counsel," instead of a formal bill of exceptions, accompanied that writ. The case is Thompson *v.* Bowne, 39 N. J. L. 2. And so the appealing party lost his just appeal because, between two different ways of saying exactly the same thing, his counsel had carelessly chosen this one instead of that. He must start afresh in his appellate proceedings and retravel the same road with a more careful eye to pitfalls.

---

[5] The systems of common law, equity, and ecclesiastical procedures.

Two persons disputed the right to some land. The question was whether defendant showed title by adverse possession. The judge, after trial without a jury, made a general finding, viz.: "I find that the plaintiff is entitled" to possession, without a statement of the facts or the legal rules on which his conclusion was based. The Supreme court, on writ of error, declined to consider the merits of the case, but affirmed the judgment, because a "finding on the blended law and facts cannot be reviewed on error." Mills v. Mott, 59 N. J. L. 15. Had counsel been sufficiently wary he would have caused the judge below to make a separate finding and statement of the facts of the case and of the rules of law applied to them. But for some cause he failed to do so and in consequence his client lost totally the right to have the judgment reviewed. Was the penalty proportioned to the offense? Is it necessary in a state system for administering justice, that the important right of review on appeal should be wholly lost for such a slip in procedure? Had it been a justice's court case, reviewed by certiorari, the court below could have been called on to certify the grounds of its decision.

A judgment having been rendered for the plaintiff after trial and verdict, defendant took the case to the Court of Errors and Appeals on writ of error. The bill of exceptions, if there was one, was not included in the printed papers of the case laid before the appellate court, and for that reason the court affirmed the judgment below without any appellate consideration of the case at all. Davis v. Littel, 64 N. J. L. 595.

A plaintiff having recovered judgment below, the Court of Errors and Appeals held that she had no right of action against the defendant. Nevertheless the court affirmed the judgment upon the ground (as to which the judges were equally divided in opinion) that defendant had not made his objection to the trial judge with sufficient definiteness. He had asked the trial judge to charge that plaintiff had "not made out any cause of action" (p. 398), which the judge declined to do. Defendant excepted, stating, in his bill of exceptions, the request and the words of the charge as actually made. One-half of the judges in the appellate court held that this exception was not sufficiently specific, and, therefore, the judgment was affirmed. The plaintiff, who had no right of action, was permitted to maintain her action. In the circumstances of that case it is probable that justice was done; for the right of action was in the plaintiff's husband, and he appears to have been assisting her in the suit. Very possibly it was his suit brought (by mistake) in her name. But mark the principle of the decision. The case was Garretson v. Appleton, 58 N. J. L. 386.

Contrast with such a system of appellate procedure, that which England has substituted for her old procedure, once essentially the same as ours. In the first place, there is no room for doubt as to the court to which the appeal should be made. All appeals from the county courts are made to the "High Court of Justice" and will be heard in the proper division of that court. All appeals from either division of the High court are to the Court of Appeals, and all appeals from the latter are to the House of Lords.[6] Appeals from decisions of a single judge of the High court go, in some cases, to a Divisional court, and in others to the Court of Appeal; but there is never a loss of the appeal because of a wrong choice in such case, and the appellate procedure is so simple and speedy that there can be but little loss of time from a mistaken choice, if it ever occurs. In the second place, the Court of Appeal has all the jurisdiction of the court below so far as may be necessary to finally determine the contest on appeal,[7] and it is required to render the judgment which the court below ought to have rendered. It may, in its discretion, receive new evidence, orally or by deposition.[8] It does not, in common-law cases, decide disputed questions of fact, for the jury trial there, as here, is regarded as a constitutional right. If a material question of fact, in real and not nominal dispute, must be determined before judgment can be rendered in such a case, a new trial is ordered,[9] but otherwise the Court of Appeal enters judgment for the party who is entitled to it according to the substantive rights of the litigants upon the facts as found and laid before the appellate court in the record or evidence. When the appeal is from the decision of a judge who has tried the case without a jury, his decision, upon the facts as well as upon the

---

[6] The appellate proceedings here considered are in civil cases in the general system of courts. The remarks do not apply to criminal cases or to cases in special local courts.

[7] Judicature Act (1873), sec. 19; and Order 58, rule 4.

[8] Order 58, rule 4.

[9] Order 58, rule 5. The Court of Appeal has held that it has power to enter judgment against the verdict where no further evidence can be offered and the verdict is clearly against evidence. Allcock v. Hall (1891), 1 Q. B. 448, and cases there cited. And see Order 40, rule 10, giving the court power to draw inferences of fact; and Annual Practice (1901), p. 823.

law, may be reviewed.[10] "All appeals" are "by way of rehearing."[11] The appellate procedure is of the simplest, and is the same in every kind of civil suit. A fourteen-day notice of appeal must be given by the appellant to his adversary to review a judgment; the record of the case with so much of the evidence as may be necessary to determine the questions in dispute is printed, and the case then takes its turn upon the docket of the appellate court.[12]

The Court of Appeal, in April, 1902, was about one year in arrear. But a bill was introduced in Parliament that summer by the government, and has since passed, to so readjust the organization and division of labor in that court as to enable it to dispose promptly of the cases before it.[13] As to the practical working of the appellate system, I have not been able to find (and I have carefully looked for) a single case in the appellate court which has miscarried; that is to say, in which the appellate court has been barred by a rule of procedure from reviewing and deciding the case upon the merits, if the court below had jurisdiction of the subject-matter. It would, of course, be intolerable to allow a negligent or crafty suitor to withhold part of his case below with the right to present it for the first time on appeal. The English system does not permit this. But the rule, fully recognized there, which in general excludes additional evidence or a "new point"[14] offered by a litigant on appeal, is not an inflexible rule stopping the court when it thinks that the offer should, in justice, be entertained. It is a matter over which the court has discretionary control, as our trial courts have over the reception of further evidence after either party has declared his case closed. And in this respect the

---

[10] Colonial Securities Co. *v.* Massey (1896), 1 Q. B. 38.

[11] "All appeals to the Court of Appeal shall be by way of rehearing, and shall be brought by notice of motion in a summary way, and no petition, case, or other formal proceeding other than such notice of motion shall be necessary." Order 58, rule 1.

[12] Order 58, rule 8.

[13] "Law Journal," Jan. 13th, and May 31st, 1902; "Law Times," Jan. 10th, 1903. The Court of Appeal, under the new act, may work in three divisions, and it has materially reduced the arrears. "Law Times," April 25th, 1903, p. 587. The third division consists of the Lord Chancellor, Chief Justice, and the presiding judge of the Probate, Divorce and Admiralty Division. They are *ex-officio* members of the Court of Appeal, but, till the act in question, rarely sat in it.

[14] Annual Practice (1901), pp. 815, 820.

English appellate court is governed by the same principle which governs our Prerogative court in its hearing of appeals.

If we look for the radical principles differentiating our system of appellate procedure in common-law courts from the present English system, they will be found in two very different fundamental conceptions respecting the nature of an appellate review of a judgment. One makes the error of the court below the object of the appellate procedure; the other takes for that object the final settlement of the controversy according to the substantive rights of the parties. These two conceptions belong to different stages of juridical civilization. In the rude judicature of the early English common-law courts, the conception of appellate procedure was that of a personal proceeding for attaint against the jury which had rendered the verdict, or for false judgment against the judge who had rendered the judgment.[15] In either case it was the wrong of the tribunal which was attacked. The contest was between the appellant and the jury or the judge who had decided against him. If he succeeded, they were punished, and severely, for the false verdict or false judgment. "The idea of a complaint against a judgment which is not an accusation against the judge is not easily formed"[16] in that age. Gradually the personal charge against the judge gave place to a charge of a specific error in his decision upon the facts as they were stated in the record, or a charge of errors which a party had committed and appearing in the record of his case. But the record did not contain the evidence. It was not till a statute, in the year 1285, introduced the bill of exceptions as a means of adding to the record the rulings of the trial court, that the evidence which gave rise to those rulings could be brought before the appellate court. Then, so much of the evidence only as related to the error specifically alleged could be examined. No question of fact could be decided; no inference of fact could be drawn by the court from the evidence. The centuries which have passed since then have seen no essential change in this method of appellate procedure in the common-law courts, as it prevails to-day in this state. In the narrow field of review to which the appellate court was confined, no difference, or but little, was made between the error that violated a substantive right of the parties and the error which violated a form of procedure; for no clear distinction was recognized between the natures of

---

[15] 2 Pol. & Mait., Histy. Engl. Law, 665.
[16] Ibid., p. 668.

the rule of procedure and the rule of substantive right. Both were equally inflexible rules of law. "False Latin," or a slip in a word or in spelling, were as fatal to a judgment[17] as a mistaken application of the law of descent. Gradually, and by piecemeal, statutory provisions permitted the courts, by amending the record, to avoid the fatal effects of most of these errors of form, and the more liberal conceptions of justice in a civilized age have introduced the judicial rule that errors of the court below, not harmful to the plaintiff in error, do not, in general, entitle him to a reversal of the judgment. But the fundamental conception still lingers in our procedure. To this day (if the court below had jurisdiction) it is only that particular error specifically pointed out and complained of in a certain narrow and technical procedure— it is that only which the appellate court can review. The question is not, What judgment ought to be rendered between these parties to finally settle, according to their substantive rights, the controversy which they have presented by their pleadings and evidence? The question is, What specific error committed by the court below is complained of in the formula prescribed by our law of procedure? The cases I have mentioned show that the effect of a slip in the steps of that procedure may be fatal to substantive rights.

The conception of complete justice as the final aim in appellate procedure, as distinguished from the correction of a particular error assigned in a technical form, is a late fruit of judicial progress. It came to the Roman law only when the latter had reached its fullest development.[18] The Church borrowed the idea from the legal procedure of Imperial Rome and incorporated it in the Canon law. Thence it found its way, in more or less

---

[17] "The precedents then set were afterwards most religiously followed to the great obstruction of justice and the ruin of the suitors; * * *. After verdicts and judgments upon the merits they were frequently reversed for slips of the pen or misspellings; and justice was perpetually entangled in a net of mere technical jargon. The legislature therefore hath been forced to interpose by no less than twelve statutes to remedy these opprobrious niceties." 3 Blackst. 410. And see Tidd's Pr., p. 826, on "Amendments;" and p. 1078, on "Error." The first of the statutes of jeofails was 14 Edw. III. (1340). A list of them is given in 18 Am. & Eng. Ency. Law, p. 475 (1st ed.).

[18] Hunter's "Roman Law", p. 1044; the appellate court could take new evidence and hear new arguments, p. 1048. For the appellate procedure in Admiralty, see Coote's Admiralty Pract. (2d ed., London), pp. 166, 167; Benedict's American Admiralty (3d ed.), §§ 615, 618.

modified forms, into those English courts whose procedure was derived from the Civil and Canon law, namely, the ecclesiastical courts and courts of admiralty and equity. Hence we find, strangely enough, in a nation as compactly organized as was the English a hundred years ago, an appellate procedure, in civil cases, highly technical and narrow in one class of its courts and broadly liberal in another. The same phenomenon of maladjustment in the administration of justice exists now in New Jersey. While the Supreme court and the Court of Errors and Appeals are required by our procedure to dismiss writs of error, or to affirm judgments, without consideration of the merits and upon such trivial points of procedure as the foregoing cases display, the Prerogative court is permitted, upon an appeal, to review the whole case and even to take further evidence,[19] if it deems it just to do so, in order to render the judgment which shall finally adjust the substantive rights of the parties. The present English appellate procedure has simply adopted the principles long familiar in the ecclesiastical and admiralty courts.[20]

---

[19] Personnett *v.* Hood, 40 N. J. E. 173.

[20] This chapter was the last of the series of articles on "Antiquated Courts." The next chapter was written more than a year later, as the first article in the second series mentioned in the preface.

CHAPTER XIV.

English Experience in Piecemeal Reform, from the Common-Law and Chancery Procedure Acts to the Judicature Act.

In an inquiry into the best method of bettering our judicial system, the main question arising at the threshold is, whether we shall retain and merely prune our ancient three-fold system of separate jurisdictions and distinct procedures (law, equity, and probate), or whether we shall consolidate them into one jurisdiction, to be exercised in one form of procedure. The latter course does not involve the consolidation of law and equity jurisprudence, but of legal and equitable jurisdiction, which is a very different thing. Not the rules of substantive rights, legal and equitable, but the powers of the courts to administer those different rights, would be unified. The rights themselves, with few exceptions, would remain distinct as before.[1]

---

[1] Of course, the procedure in legal and equitable cases cannot be in all points identical. In the enforcement of distinct legal and equitable rights there is, in the unified system, but one form of action and one general course of procedure; with different modes of trial, however, for legal and equitable cases, and with such other differences in steps in the cause as may be appropriate to the different modes of trial, or required for the peculiar nature of the different cases. The distinction is stated by Prof. Pomeroy thus: "The codes of procedure do not attempt to effect so radical and sweeping an alteration (as the consolidation of legal and equitable substantive rights); the distinctions between law and equity are not abolished; these two departments of the municipal law, comprising their distinctive and peculiar rights and duties and furnishing their special remedies, are left untouched by the legislation, and it is plain that they cannot be consolidated into one so long as the jury trial is preserved and made compulsory." But "all distinctions between the action formerly used to enforce equitable rights and to obtain equitable remedies" (as an injunction, or decree for specific performance, and the like), "and those formerly used to enforce legal rights and obtain legal remedies, are removed; and one judicial proceeding, with the same essential principles and features, is to be used in enforcing all species of rights and obtaining all kinds of remedies." "Code Remedies," Sec. 36. He recognizes the fact that the unification of procedure cannot be complete "As long as the jury trial lasts in civil cases   *   *   *   an absolute identity in the mode of trial is plainly

Neither does this course necessarily involve the administration of law, equity and probate by the same judges. A different set of judges, sitting separately, may be assigned to hear cases belonging to each of those respective classes; but each set would have the power to hear all classes of cases. That is the practice in England and Ontario. The advantage of such a system is that a case involving both legal and equitable rights, as a suit to restrain a nuisance and to recover damages for it, need not be split into two actions; and a law case which, by mistake, might be brought before equity judges, would not, for that reason, be dismissed, but would either be transferred, in its present stage, to the appropriate bench to proceed without change of pleadings; or for proper cause, in the discretion of the court, it could be retained and heard on its merits by the judges before whom it was first brought, a jury being impaneled, if demanded.

Neither does this course involve necessarily the adoption of a code of procedure, in the American sense of that term. For Connecticut has adopted this system, in the main, but that state has no code of procedure. Neither has England nor Canada.

The English tried the course of piecemeal improvement and readjustment of the triple system, and after about twenty years' experience abandoned it for the unified system. With the latter, English professional and public opinion appears to be pretty well satisfied after thirty years' trial.

The great agitation for legal and political reform that preceded the Reform Bill of 1832 effected but little change in legal procedure at that time. Lord Eldon's Commission (1826) recommended almost nothing by way of large reform in the Chancery procedure.[2] The reports of the Royal Commissioners, made in 1829, 1830, 1831 and 1832, dealt entirely with details in the

---

impracticable; and this difference is so important, so vital, that it extends through the whole frame-work of actions and separates them into two distinctive classes, notwithstanding the positive and sweeping language of the statute which purports to abolish all distinctions and forms, and to prescribe one uniform mode or instrument for the procurement of all remedies." Ibid., Sec. 59. And see also Sec. 23, 68, 70.

[2] "Report of Commissioners to Inquire into the Practice of the Court of Chancery" (Lord Eldon, Chairman); dated Feb. 28th, 1826. All of the English Reports of Commissioners mentioned in this article may be seen in the Library of the New York City Bar Association. Some of them are also in the Library of "The Law Institute," in the New York Post Office building.

Common law procedure.[3] They proposed many of the changes which were adopted twenty years later in the Common Law Procedure Acts, but the conservative sentiment of the profession would not yield to them in 1832, and that stage of the movement for reform ended with two statutes[4] improving the methods of beginning actions and some other features of detail, and conferring on the law courts the authority under which they made the "Hilary Rules," in 1834. These rules, which have not been adopted in New Jersey, made important modifications within a narrow range of procedure, notably in the use of the common counts and the general issue in pleading, but fell far short of the reform specifically recommended by the Commissioners. According to Sir Frederick Pollock, the rules were "a lame and unhappy compromise."[5]

The twenty years following the Reform Act were a period of great social, administrative and political reforms. The tide of change was in full flood. In the form of the Democratic Movement—which was essentially a criticism of the old order—it swept over the continent of Europe, Great Britain and the United States. The same year—1848—saw the introduction of the Code of Civil Procedure in this country, the abolition of the Corn Laws of England, and the great political revolutions of the continent. Very great changes in substantive and administrative law were made in England in that period, and the rapid industrial development of the country brought upon the Court of

---

[3] "Reports of the Commissioners on the Practice and Pleadings of the English Common Law Courts," 1829-1834.

[4] "An Act for Uniformity of Process in Personal Actions in his Majesty's Courts of Law at Westminster;" 2 W. IV, c. 39 (May 23d, 1832), 72 St. at Large, p. 115. The act contains twenty-three sections.

"An Act for the further Amendment of the Law and the better Advancement of Justice;" 3 & 4 W. IV, c. 42 (Aug. 14th, 1833). The act contains forty-five sections. It empowers the courts of law "by any rule or order" to make alterations in the modes of pleading, et cet. It also made many changes in details of procedure, from which a few afterward found their way, in different forms, into our statutes; e. g. the use of the initials of Christian names in suing on written instruments in certain cases, authority to the courts to make rules respecting the proof and inspection of documents, et cet.

Both the last above mentioned acts and the "Hilary Rules" are given in full in the Appendix to 1 Chitty's Pleadings, pp. 703-747.

[5] In an article by him, "The Law of England, I-L Victoriae," 3 Law Quart. Rev. (1887), p. 342.

Chancery a volume of business which it was totally unable, fettered by the old procedure, to keep up with. Speaking of the Court of Chancery as it was in 1852, the biographer of Lord Chancellor Westbury says: "Its business had doubled during the past thirty years. * * * Popular writers and public speakers covered the Court of Chancery with ridicule, but seven judges now failed to satisfy the requirements of the constantly increasing number of suitors who resorted to it."[6]

The unsatisfactory conditions of judicial business and judicial procedure, and the great advance in public sentiment for making changes in the old order of things, brought about the appointment, in 1850, of the Common Law Commissioners and of the Chancery Commissioners for the purpose of again making separate inquiries into the common law and chancery procedures.[7]

The first and second reports of the Common Law Commissioners (1851, 1853) led to the two Common Law Procedure Acts of 1852 and 1854. From these statutes were taken most or all of the provisions of our "Act to simplify the pleadings and practice in courts of law," passed in 1855 and embodied in ninety sections (121 to 210) of our Practice Act, in Nixon's Digest (edition of 1868, p. 733). They included our present Ejectment Act. Nearly all the provisions of the act of 1855 are still in our law of procedure.

The Common Law Procedure Acts, however, in several important particulars, went much farther than our reform. The first act[8] provided that "causes of action of whatever kind, provided they be by and against the same parties and in the same rights, may be joined in the same suit," except replevin and ejectment; but the court could order separate trials (Sec. 41). By consent, trial could be had, without pleadings, on an issue to be stated in writing (Sec.

---

[6] "Life of Richard Lord Westbury," by Thomas A. Nash (London, 1888), Vol. I, p. 120. The seven judges were, the Chancellor, Master of the Rolls, three Vice-Chancellors, and two judges of the Court of Chancery Appeals. At the page cited is given a good description of the procedure in Chancery in 1852, which is almost as bad as Dickens describes it in "Bleak House." But the business of the law courts had declined; Finlason's "Exposition of our Judicial System," p. 27.

[7] "Reports of Commissioners appointed to inquire into the Practice and Pleadings of the Superior Courts of Common Law." (1851-53-60).

[8] "An Act to amend the Process, Practice and Mode of Pleading in the Superior Courts of Common Law," et cet, 15 & 16 Vic., c. 76 (June 30th, 1852), 92 St. at Large, p. 444. It contains two hundred and thirty-six sections.

42). All statements which need not be proved, including promises on indebitatus counts, must be omitted from the pleadings, and the forms of declarations and pleas were very much simplified.[9] Writs of error in civil actions were abolished, and "proceedings in error" were made "a step in the cause;" they were begun by a written "memorandum" alleging error in law, which, with a "statement of the grounds of error," was served on the adverse party (Sec. 148, 149). The writ of summons was put into the rational form still used in England, namely, a warning to defendant to enter an appearance within a stated time, and that in default of doing so plaintiff could take judgment. (Schedule A, No. 1, of forms.)

The second act[10] allowed appeals from a refusal to grant a new trial, in certain cases (Sec. 35); permitted the plaintiff, in any action except replevin and ejectment, to claim a writ of mandamus commanding defendant to fulfil any duty in the fulfilment of which the plaintiff is personally interested" (Sec. 68, 69); and prescribed the frame of the declaration, which was limited to cases in which the plaintiff would "sustain damage" by the nonperformance of the duty; permitted the plaintiff to claim, in addition to damages, a writ of injunction, in any action for "breach of contract or other injury," against the "repetition or continuance" of the wrong (Sec. 79); permitted defendant to plead equitable defenses (Sec. 83).

The long and exhaustive reports of the Commissioners who recommended these reforms went even farther than these acts. They had before them

---

[9] Sections 60, 67 79, 89; Schedule B of forms of pleading. Under the first Common Law Procedure Act the pleadings upon an overdue promissory note, with payment as a defense, would have been as follows: DECLARATION: A B, by E F, his attorney, sues C D for that the defendant on the —— day of ——, by his promissory note, now overdue, promised to pay to the plaintiff £100 two months after date, but did not pay the same. And the plaintiff claims £100 and interest. (Schedule B, No. 15.) PLEA: The defendant, by X, his attorney, says that before the action he satisfied and discharged the plaintiff's claim by payment. (Id., Nos. 34, 40.) Contrast these forms with the grotesque jargon still used by us—in the Twentieth Century.

[10] "An Act for the further amendment of the Process, Practice and Mode of Pleading," et cet., 17 & 18 Vic., c. 125 (Aug. 12th, 1854), 94 St. at Large, p. 794. It contains one hundred and seven sections.

evidence of the working of the New York code of civil procedure,[11] and the Commissioners so far expressed their "opinion upon what is commonly called the fusion of law and equity as to say that * * * the courts of common law, to be able satisfactorily to administer justice, ought to possess, in all matters within their jurisdiction, the power to give all the redress necessary to protect and vindicate common law rights and to prevent wrong, whether existing or likely to happen unless prevented." (Second report, April 30, 1853, p. 53.) In the opinion of Sir Frederick Pollock, the reforms of the Common Law Procedure Acts which followed these reports "were wise and sagacious in what they accomplished and in what they left undone for the time being. For over twenty years they did good service."[12]

The final report of these Commissioners (1860) stated that the practice was satisfactorily improved by these acts, proposed some further improvements, and strongly recommended enlarging yet more the chancery powers of the law courts. (Third report, p. 8.) This report was followed by the third Common Law Procedure Act (1860),[13] giving law courts the power to relieve against forfeitures in certain cases, but not otherwise enlarging much their jurisdiction.

The Chancery Commissioners made three reports, in 1852, 1854 and 1856.[14] The first pointed out that the mischiefs arising from a "system of several distinct courts proceeding on distinct, and in some cases on antagonistic principles, are extensive and deep rooted" (page 1). It mentioned, as defects in the judicial system, that the law courts cannot preserve the

---

[11] "Evidence on the Operation of the Code obtained by the English Law Amendment Society and Chancery Commission, and published in England. Republished from the Law Review and Commissioners' Report and presented to Parliament" (N. Y., 1852). In "Law Reform Tracts," Vol. 8, Pamphlets, Library of N. Y. City Bar Assn. It appears in this publication that David Dudley Field testified before the English Chancery Commissioners and produced letters from a number of New York judges as to practical working of the code.

[12] Same article mentioned in note 5 above.

[13] "An Act for the further Amendment of the Process, Practice and Mode of Pleading in, and enlarging the Jurisdiction of, the Superior Courts of Common Law." 23 & 24 Vic., c. 126 (Aug. 28th, 1860), 100 St. at Large, p. 670.

[14] Reports of the English Chancery Commissioners, 1852-54-56. The improvements in Chancery procedure prior to 1852 (namely in 1828, 1840 and 1845) were relatively so inconsiderable that I have not taken space to describe them. They are referred to in the article of Mr. Daniel, mentioned in note 19.

property involved in litigation before them; that parties are sent back and forth from one court to another in one case; that equity courts will not decide questions of law; that these proceedings are abused to cause delay; that parties lose their cases because eminent counsel mistake the proper court of remedy; that "the misfortune to suitors in the Court of Chancery is * * * that the expense of the protection afforded often absorbs the whole amount of the property protected" (p. 11).[15] The report stated that suggestion had been made to abolish the "distinction between law and equity" and to "blend the courts into one court of universal jurisdiction," but the report pointed out difficulties in that course. It recommended that the "jurisdiction now exercised by courts of equity may be conferred on courts of law, and that the jurisdiction now exercised by courts of law may be exercised by courts of equity" * * * (p. 3). The report contained recommendations for many specific reforms in details of chancery procedure.

The report was followed by the "Act to amend the Practice and Course of Proceedings in the High Court of Chancery"[16] (July 1, 1852), which, according to the biographer of Lord Westbury, "revolutionized the equity system."[17] Among the changes were these: Writs of subpœna to answer were abolished; suits must be begun by serving a printed copy of the bill of complaint, endorsed with a notice in the nature of a summons; interrogatories could be filed separately by either side (Sec. 11-19); the old practice of examining witnesses was abolished, and testimony could be taken orally before an examiner, who must reduce it to writing, in the presence of counsel, on both sides, and transmit it, signed by the witnesses, to the court (Sec. 28-32); the examiner could not rule on objections to the evidence; the Court of Chancery must decide all questions of law and all legal rights arising in the course of an equity suit, and was prohibited from requiring parties to proceed at law to determine such questions. (Sec. 61, 62.)

---

[15] Dickens mentions some gross instances in the preface to "Bleak House," which are no worse than cases shown in this Report. "Bleak House" was published in 1852-1853.

[16] 15 & 16 Vic., c. 86, 92 St. at Large, p. 454. It contains sixty-seven sections. As part of the same reform Parliament passed, on the previous day (June 3oth). "An act to abolish the office of Master in Ordinary of the High Court of Chancery and to make provision for the more speedy and efficient dispatch of business in the said court." 15 & 16 Vic., c. 80, 92 St. at Large, p. 363.

[17] Life of Lord Westbury, Vol. I, p. 124.

After this, act was passed the Commissioners made a second report dealing entirely with subjects pertaining to the Ecclesiastical courts.

The third report of the Chancery Commissioners (1856) recommended enlarging the law powers of the equity courts to allow them to assess damages in injunction cases, to ascertain damages in suits for specific performance and to frame issues and submit them to a jury in such cases. Both this report and that of the Chancery Evidence Commission (appointed 1859, report dated 1860) criticized the method of taking evidence orally before examiners, and the latter report recommended that evidence upon disputed facts be taken orally before the court. But this latter recommendation was not enacted by Parliament.

These several procedure acts "but whetted the appetites of the advocates of a complete reorganization" of the judicial system. Sir Richard Bethell (afterward Lord Westbury), as Solicitor General, declared in Parliament that he would never rest content till that should be effected "without which all law reform would prove ineffectual—the consolidation of jurisdiction and the administration of equity and common law from the same bench."[18] The Procedure Acts were a step forward and temporarily relieved the Situation, but the lack of unity inherent in the old triple system of procedure was an insuperable obstacle to any adequate adjustment of the judicial machinery to the increased work brought to it by the enormous development of all forms of social activity. The agitation for consolidation continued; the arrears of the courts accumulated;[19] in 1867 a new commission of inquiry into the whole judicature system was appointed, and the resulting report brought the Judicature Act of 1873.

Mr. W. F. Finlason's book,[20] published in 1877, gives a good description of the helplessness of the English courts in 1873. In his opinion, "prior to the Judicature Act there was, indeed, no judicial system in this country; there were

---

[18] Ibid, pp. 124, 133.

[19] See a paper by Mr. W. T. S. Daniel, Q. C., on "Recent Reforms in the Court of Chancery," in "Transactions of the National Association for the Promotion of Social Science," 1859, p. 169, and other papers by the same and other authors on the "Reorganization of the Courts," in the "Transactions" for 1868, pp. 205, 225.

[20] "An Exposition of Our Judicial System and Civil Procedure as reconstructed under the Judicature Acts, including the act of 1876, with Comments on their Effect and Operation." By W. F. Finlason (London, 1877).

isolated institutions, some of which might be termed systems more or less complete, but all of them separate and unconnected" (p. 3). He says that after the Common Law Procedure Acts, "the evil practice of setting aside verdicts and sending cases to new trial increased;" "the largest portion of the time of the Courts of Common Law was taken up in hearing applications for new trials, and the arrears were enormous" (p. 28). He quotes Mr. Justice Maule as saying that "Of all the modes ever invented of administering justice, that of an application for a new trial was incomparably the worst" (p. 359). He says that the block and delay in the Chancery courts (partly due to the then recent abolition of the offices of master) led to the appointment of the Judicature Commission in 1867.

That Commission included representatives from the law and equity benches and from the bar—sixteen or more of them in all. Among them were Lord Chancellor Cairns, Vice-Chancellor Wood, Sir Roundel Palmer (afterward Lord Chancellor Selborne), Mr. Justice Blackburn, Mr. Justice Smith. They were appointed "to inquire into the operation and effect of the present constitution of" the Courts of Law and Equity and the Ecclesiastical courts. Their first report,[21] dated March 25, 1869, stated that the Court of Chancery was then bound to decide questions of law arising in it and to assess damages, and that the jury had been introduced into it; that the court of law were empowered to compel discovery; that they had limited power to grant injunctions; that they could allow equitable defenses and in certain cases could grant relief from forfeitures. These changes, the report stated, caused "considerable improvement," but after many years' experience and careful consideration the commissioners were of opinion "that the transfer or blending of jurisdiction attempted to be carried out by recent acts of Parliament, even if it had been adopted to the full extent recommended by the Commissioners, is not a sufficient or adequate remedy for the evils complained of, and would at best have mitigated, but not removed, the most prominent of those evils." The report stated that the right to claim an injunction and to plead equitable defenses, in the law courts, had not been of much use; trial by jury, in chancery, was also not much used; that the mischiefs cannot "be completely remedied by any mere transfer or blending of

---

[21] Reports of the English Judicature Commissioners, 1869-1874.

jurisdiction between the courts as at present constituted, and that the first step toward meeting and surmounting the evils complained of will be the consolidation of all the superior courts of law and equity, together with the courts of probate, divorce and admiralty, into one court, to be called 'Her Majesty's Supreme Court,' in which court shall be vested all the jurisdiction which is now exercisable by each and all the courts so consolidated" (p. 9). It recommended that the Supreme court be divided into divisions of the Queen's Bench, Chancery, etc.

Respecting procedure, the report stated that there should be as much uniformity in it as is consistent with the principle of making the procedure in each division of the court appropriate to the nature of the classes of cases assigned to it (p.10). The report considered the defects of both the common law and equity pleadings, and concluded, that "the best system would be one which combined the comparative brevity of the simpler forms of common law pleading with the principle of stating intelligently, and not technically, the substance of the facts relied upon as constituting the plaintiff's or defendant's case, as distinguished from his evidence;" "it is upon this principle that most modern improvements of pleading have been founded, both in the United States and in our own colonies and Indian possessions and in the practice recently settled for the courts of probate and divorce" (p. 11).

In order to prevent litigation for delay, the report advised that in suits on contracts for specified sums of money, as on negotiable instruments, on ordinary accounts and the like, the plaintiff should be entitled, on affidavit that the full amount is due, to an order to show cause why judgment should not be entered, notwithstanding defendant had appeared to defend the action (p. 11).

As to parties, the report recommended that any person having such an interest as to make his presence expedient "should be summoned to attend the further proceedings and should be bound thereby," and to this end the plaintiff should be entitled, on application and an order, to bring in any third person against whom he may think he is entitled to relief; as in cases where defendant claims contribution. The report considered the different modes of trial and stated that in common-law cases a "jury has always been regarded as a constitutional tribunal for trying issues of fact;" it recommended that the judge should be empowered to order the parties to prepare and define the issues for trial, and if they cannot agree, that he should settle them himself; that evidence be taken orally in open court (this was then new in chancery cases), subject to the court's order, that any matter, at any time, might be proved by affidavit, or before a commissioner or examiner, or on interrogatories; that parties might be required, in the court's discretion, to admit specific facts, or pay the cost of proving them (p. 15); that, on a motion for a new trial, the court should be able to enter a verdict or a nonsuit; that costs should in all cases be in the discretion of the court.

The report gave much space to the consideration of the then existing appellate system. It mentioned as one of the objections to the review of judgments in the Exchequer Chamber that "the judges who have been overruled to-day, may tomorrow themselves sit in appeal from some decision of the judges who have taken part in overruling them."[22] It recommended the establishment of a Court of Appeal as a part or a division of the Supreme court; that proceedings in error and on bills of exception be abolished, and a mere notice of appeal, without petition, be substituted, except in appeals to the House of Lords, in which a petition should be used; that every appeal should be "in the nature of a rehearing," and that the Court of Appeal should be empowered to amend or supplement the pleadings, to admit further evidence, and that in all cases it should have jurisdiction over the whole record, with power to vary the order or judgment (p. 24).

The second report (July 3, 1872) of the Commissioners (to whom Lord Chancellor Hatherly, Mr. Justice Wills and others had, in the meantime, been added) deals with the county, and other inferior, courts. The Commissioners "recommend that county courts should be annexed to and form constituent parts or branches of the proposed high court of justice" (p. 13). At that time, as the report shows, the common-law jurisdiction of the county courts was limited to £50 value, while they had equity jurisdiction in some cases to the value of £500. The Commissioners recommended that the jurisdiction of the county courts should be unlimited, but subject to the power of transfer to the high court when the value involved exceeds £50, on application of either party or on the judge's own motion.

---

[22] The Court of Exchequer Chamber consisted of all the judges of the Courts of King's Bench, Common Pleas and Exchequer, sitting under such arrangements that errors in any one of those courts were heard by the judges of the others.

The third, fourth and fifth reports were all made in 1874, after the Judicature Act had been passed, but before it took effect. They were very short. The third dealt with the subject of "Tribunals of Commerce," recommending that they be established; the fourth dealt with the subject of making uniform the practice at chambers under the new Judicature Act; the fifth and final report dealt with the proposed appointment of "public prosecutors," and other matters connected with the assizes, criminal courts, and the disposal of civil business in certain counties.

The recommendations above mentioned respecting the county courts and Tribunals of Commerce have not been adopted by Parliament, and there was much controversy among the judges over the recommendations of the Commissioners respecting the superior courts.[23] About four years elapsed before Parliament enacted the Judicature Act (1873), by which the principles and most of the details recommended in the first report were adopted.[24]

The act was passed under the lead of Lord Chancellor Selborne in the House of Lords, and Lord Coleridge in the House of Commons. It took effect November 1, 1875.

---

[23] Finlason, "Exposition of Our Judicial System," pp. 52, 55.
[24] See chap. VII, *ante*, describing the English system of courts under the Judicature Act.

CHAPTER XV.

THE PRACTICAL WORKING OF THE ENGLISH JUDICATURE ACTS.

The first few years' experience of the working of the Judicature Act (1873) was not at all satisfactory. Some of the difficulties were doubtless inevitable in case of any radical change, however superior, in a system so highly organized and intricate as that which the new procedure supplanted.[1] Time and experience are required to adapt the habits of men to changes so profound. But some of the difficulties were caused by defects in the new system. The law periodicals, for a number of years following 1875, contain criticisms in plenty.[2] Lord Bowen, one of the judges of the Court of Appeal, complained, in 1886, of the considerable arrears in both the Queen's Bench and Chancery Divisions; of the unnecessary loss of time by the judges in Circuit work; of the tedious hearings in the Chancery Division, and of the frequent interruptions in trials there, caused by adjournments. He criticized the new methods of pleading, and thought that the machinery of litigation was too elaborate and precise; that the change caused an enormous increase in the number of appeals, and that the act tended to make the Court of Appeal "the pivot of the new system" as the "Courts of Banc were the pivot of the old."[3] At that time appeals were allowed with very little restraint, but an amendment to the act, since then, has limited very much the right of appeal from interlocutory orders.

---

[1] I have not heard of any difficulty attending upon the introduction of the new procedure in Connecticut.

[2] The following references will give a fair notion of the criticisms: Preface to Finlason's "Exposition of our Judicial System" (1877); "The Judicature Act," 4 L. Mag. & Rev. (N. S.), [1875] p. 538; Comments on the Working of the Act in 20 Solrs.' Jour. & Rep. 821, 840; "The Procedure of the High Court of Justice," by Alfred Hill, 19th Century (1883), Vol. 13, p. 105; Preface to first edition of W. B. Odger's "Procedure, Pleading and Practice."

[3] "The Law Courts under the Judicature Acts." by Lord Bowen, 2 Law Quart. Rev. (1886), p. 1.

Lord Coleridge, as Attorney-General and a member of Mr. Gladstone's cabinet, had aided in passing the Judicature Act in 1873. He defended it also in Parliament after the first year of its working had provoked much opposition.[4] But later, after he had been Chief Justice of England for a time, he complained of the effect of the act in diminishing the prestige of his office. Although *ex officio* a member of the Court of Appeal, the Chief Justice did not often sit in it; and his decisions below were, of course, sometimes reversed in that tribunal. Moreover, he did not sit in the House of Lords on the hearing of appeals, where the Chancellor presided. In a letter, written in 1889, to Lord Lindley, one of the members of the Court of Appeal, he says: "I was terribly done up by the end of the circuit. * * *. To get the work done I had to sit almost always till seven and sometimes much later. * * * I have been nearly sixteen years a judge, and if I could get my full pension on the ground of permanent incapacity, I would go to-morrow. For if I could have foreseen, as perhaps I ought, how the Judicature Act would be worked, I would have resigned sooner than have been a party to it. The steady lowering of the judges of first instance and the enthroning of the Chancellor upon the necks of all of us, have altered the profession so far as the common law is concerned, and made success in it, except so far as money making is concerned, not an object of ambition to a high-minded man. It frets me more than I can tell you to feel that the great place I hold is being let down year by year, and I don't know how to prevent it."[5]

In another letter to the same correspondent, written a few days later, he says: "It is really a past feeling with me, at least I think so, to be the least jealous of the C. A. (Court of Appeal). I certainly sometimes think it wrong, though not oftener than they think me—not so often, indeed; and I know the judges are right good fellows—great lawyers, who desire the right and the true. But I think the system tends to reduce the Divisional courts to note-takers and hearers of dress rehearsals for the C. A., and this I think a great evil for the judges, as tending to render them hasty and slovenly, and for the suitor, as multiplying appeals means increased costs, which common-law actions can rarely stand."[6]

---

[4] See a statement of his argument in defense in the House of Lords, 20 Solrs.' Jour. & Rep. 805.

[5] Life and Correspondence of Lord Coleridge (London, 1904), Vol. II, p. 359.

[6] Ibid., p. 361.

The writer of the article upon the "Supreme Court" in the "Encyclopedia of the Laws of England" says that the Divisional courts have not given satisfaction, and that Mr. Justice Cave, in a memorandum, in July, 1892, upon the Report of the Council of Judges, had expressed the opinion that their business should either be transacted by one judge or be transferred to the Court of Appeal. The writer of that article also says that the Bar Committee and a committee of the Incorporated Law Society were of the same opinion.[7]

The agitation for reforms in the new system led to a recommendation by the judges to the Home Secretary, in 1892, of a number of changes in the new system, most of which have since been made.[8] To the year 1902 inclusive there had been fourteen amendatory acts (including amendments of amendments) of the first Judicature Act, containing in the aggregate 179 sections. There have also been a number of changes in the rules of court.

Pretty much all of the criticisms, and all of the amendments, have been directed to details. None of those written since the act took effect, so far as I have seen, attacked the general scheme or fundamental principles of the new system. Sir Frederick Pollock, writing in 1887, says of the Judicature Acts: "Adequate criticism is not possible for our generation. The occurrence of a certain amount of friction, the discovery of a certain number of manifest faults in the first seven or ten years' trial of so far-reaching a plan proves only that its devisers were not more than human. You cannot work a refined system of law by a uniformly cheap and speedy procedure. * * * What can be done, and recent changes have aimed at doing, is to speed and smooth the course of justice in its ordinary dealing, whether coercive or administrative, in the cases where there is no real difficulty." He is decisive, however, as to the effect of the change upon substantive law, saying, "It needs not much discourse to

---

[7] "Encyclopedia of the Laws of England" (London; Revised to 1898), Vol. 12, at p. 51. For further adverse comment on the Divisional Courts, see 45 Solrs.' Jour. (1901), p. 548. The Divisional Courts consist of any two justices of the King's Bench Division sitting to hear arguments on certain classes of matters. What we would call sittings of the K. B. in banc are held in that way only, not more than two judges sitting together. The Divisional Courts are intermediate courts of appeal between courts held by single judges, and the Court of Appeal. See Appendix I, § 40; II, Order LIX.

[8] "English Law Reform." The Juridical Rev. (1892), Vol. 4, p. 335.

show that as to the substance of the law the result of the Judicature Acts has been clear gain."⁹

Criticism at present appears to be confined to such details as the organization of the circuit system which is said to take, needlessly, much time of the judges; and to the inadequacy of the present force of judges to cope with the increasing volume of business. I have found nothing in the law periodicals of the last five years directed against the regulations which govern the steps in the cause, or the methods of administering relief.[10] Doubtless the process of gradual improvement will continue in these respects also; but even in the present stage of that process, my research tends to confirm the following estimate by Mr. W. B. Odgers, a practicing barrister and a well-recognized authority upon English procedure. In a lecture delivered in London in 1901, he said: "No honest litigant of ordinary sagacity can now be defeated in an action by any mere technicality, or lose his case through any mistaken Step or accidental slip."[11]

The English judges have contributed their share to the success of the reforms by their liberal and enlightened interpretation of the Judicature Acts. Some illustration of this Spirit may be found in the following excerpts from judicial decisions: "The main object of the Judicature Act was to enable the parties to a suit to obtain in that suit, and without the necessity of resorting to another court, all remedies to which they are entitled in respect of any legal or equitable claim or defense properly advanced by them, so as to avoid a multiplicity of legal proceedings."[12]

---

[9] "The Law of England, I-L Victoriae" (3 Law Quart. Rev. [1887] 342, 346), by Sir F. Pollock.

[10] I have searched the indexes and tables of contents of the several volumes of the following English periodicals for the years 1900-1904, inclusive: "Juridical Review," "Law Journal," "Law Magazine and Review," "Solicitors' Journal." And although there was, in nearly, or quite every volume, discussion of the need for reforming the circuit system, for increasing the judicial force on the bench, and for improving the county courts system, I found no complaint of the working of the Judicature Acts in other respects, except that of a speaker at a meeting of "The Solicitors' Managing Clerks' Association," whose remarks are reported in 46 Solicitors' Journal (1902), p. 411.

[11] W. Blake Odgers, in "A Century of Law Reform" (Macmillan, London, 1901), p. 240. Mr. Odgers is the author of "Procedure, Pleading and Practice" under the Judicature Acts, the fifth edition of which appeared in 1903.

[12] Lord Watson in Ind. *v.* Emerson, 12 App. Cas. (House of Lords), 300, 308 [1887].

"The great object of the Court of Appeal has been to make litigation as short, as cheap, and as safe for the suitors as practicable. * * * Every endeavor has been made to carry out this principle," (of section 25 (7) of the Judicature Act (1873), providing that the courts should grant, in the one suit, all legal and equitable remedies in order to completely settle the controversy and avoid multiplicity of legal proceedings), "and all the judges have tried to bring litigation to an end as speedily as possible."[13]

The volume of work performed by the courts, under the Judicature Acts, is very large. A full and classified account of it is published yearly under the title "Judicial Statistics." Sir John Macdonell, a master of the court, edits the work.[14] I take the following figures from the volume for 1902, published in 1904. In reading them, it should be remembered that the working force of

The Chancery Division of the "High Court" is	6	judges.
The King's Bench Division of the "High Court" is	15	"
The Probate, Divorce and Admiralty Div. is	2	"
Total judges of first instance in "High Court"	23	"

Under the heading "High Court of Justice—Chancery Division," Table XII, (p. 66), shows the "Number and disposal of actions for trial," as follows, for the year 1902:

ACTIONS PENDING FOR HEARING.

Pending at commencement of year	140
Set down during the year	1060
	1200

ACTIONS DISPOSED OF.

Heard and determined:

---

[13] Brett, M. R., in McGowan *v.* Middleton (1883), in the Court of Appeal, 11 Q. B., p. 468.

[14] "Judicial Statistics, England and Wales. 1902." "Part II. Civil Judicial Statistics." (London, 1904.) Price, 2s. 1d. It is an official publication.

Witness actions	532	
Nonwitness actions	70	
	602	
Otherwise disposed of	472	
	1074	
Actions pending at end of year	126	
		1200

The foregoing work was done by the six judges of the Chancery Division. There were, however, other matters heard by those judges, for in the summary of the work of all the courts, stated below, the total of matters "heard and determined" in the Chancery Division is stated to be 838.

Under the heading "King's Bench Division," Table, XXIII, (p. 76), shows the "Number and disposal of actions for trial" as follows, for the year 1902:

ACTIONS TRIED OR OTHERWISE DISPOSED OF IN COURT.

Actions defended:		
Before a special jury	745	
" common jury	727	
" judge without jury	1007	
" official referees	196	
Total defended		2675
Actions undefended:		
Before a special jury	10	
" common jury	39	
" judge without jury	90	
" official referee	3	
		142
Total tried, etc., in court		2817

In addition there were argued before the judges of that court, sitting as Divisional Courts, appeals from inferior courts (p. 92)	251

Additional matters (including matters—not being appeals from inferior courts—in the Divisional Courts) "heard and determined" by these judges, bring the total to 3,513. This work was done by the fifteen judges of the King's Bench Division and includes their work at circuit.

Motions for new trials are not separated, in the statistics, from "Motions for judgment." Both are made in the Court of Appeal. (Orders 39, 40.) Verdicts often find the disputed facts specially and judgment is entered thereon by the trial judge. Either side may then move in the Court of Appeal to set aside the judgment and enter any other judgment warranted by the facts as found. That motion is a motion for judgment. Or he may move in that court merely for a new trial. The number of "Motions for new trials or to enter judgment" for the year 1902 was (p. 16).

		Annual average, 1898-1902.
Allowed	33	
Dismissed	50	78
Varied	3	
Withdrawn	26	17
Struck out	9	
	121	95

The Court of Appeal granted only nine new trials in 1902, according to the letter of Mr. Crane, presently mentioned. In the 40th volume of Vroom's Reports there were 18 new trials reported as granted, and 8 refused, in our Supreme court, on rules to show cause, during the two terms of February and June, 1903.

Besides their work in trying cases, the fifteen judges of the King's Bench Division take turns in sitting in the Divisional courts. These courts hear appeals from Inferior courts, and from decisions of the Masters and of single judges of the King's Bench Division of the High court.

On page 17 of the "Judicial Statistics" is a summary of the work done by all the courts of England and Wales.

From this it appears that the twenty-three judges of the High court (including all its divisions) did the following work as judges of first instance:

COURTS OF FIRST INSTANCE: HIGH COURT OF JUSTICE:	Actions, etc., heard and determined.	
	Year 1902.	Annual Average, 1898-1902.
Chancery Division	838	884
King's Bench Division	3513	3616
Probate Actions	103	115
Divorce and Matrimonial Suits	734	636
Admiralty Actions	263	250
Lunacy	132	142
Railway and Canal Commission	28	41
	5611	5684

Appeals "heard and determined" in the House of Lordsand Court of Appeal were:

House of Lords	49	52
Court of Appeal	618	597

The average time between setting down appeals and the time of disposing of them in the Court of Appeal was (p. 21):

Appeals from Chancery Division	217 days.
" " King's Bench Division	154 "

The average time between issue joined and trial of causes is not stated in the "Judicial Statistics;" but in a letter written in 1903 by its editor and published in the Report of the "Laws Delay Commission" of New York, presently to be mentioned, it appears that, (pp. 94, 101 of that Report) "the period varies from three to six months, and is as a rule nearer the former than the latter. As to cases tried on circuit the interval may be much shorter; it may be, if the circuits are near when issue is joined, only a fortnight; or, if 'short notice of trial,' or 'any notice of trial' is allowed, the interval between issue joined and trial may be only a few days."

The "Laws Delay Commission," consisting of Wheeler H. Peckham, Edward Lauterbach, Lawrence Godkin, Horatio C. King, Edmund Wetmore, Robert E. Deyo, and H. B. Hepburn, reported in January, 1904, to the Governor of New York upon the congestion of business in the courts in the counties of Kings and of New York.[15] The report gives a good deal of consideration to the English system. Through Ambassador Choate, the commission received letters of information from Sir John Macdonell, editor of "Judicial Statistics," from Mr. Justice Bigham, of the High court, and from Mr. T. Newton Crane, a practicing barrister in England.[16] The commission recommends the adoption of several features of the English system: among them, (1) provision for compelling the parties to a litigated action to appear before a Supreme court commissioner (a master, in England) to determine all preliminary questions prior to trial; this to include all matters now the subject of special motions; (2) provision for a summary inquiry at plaintiff's option by a master (Supreme court commissioner) into the merits of the defense in any action on contract for a sum certain, and for entry of judgment forthwith in such cases if the defense is a sham, or for leave to defend on conditions imposed by the master (subject to appeal to a judge) if the defense is suspicious; (3) the keeping and publication of judicial statistics for the state.[17]

---

[15] "Report of the Commission on Law's Delay." Transmitted to the Legislature Jan. 25, 1904.

[16] The letters are printed in full in the appendix to the Report, page 94 *et seq.*

[17] Report, pp. 65, 66, 70. I am indebted to the courtesy of Mr. J. Noble Hayes, counsel to the Commission, for a copy of the report, and for an opportunity to examine his copy of the "Judicial Statistics," from which I have quoted in this article.

CHAPTER XVI.

THE PRINCIPLES OF THE ENGLISH PROCEDURE.

The Governor has recently (May, 1905) appointed the Commission to inquire and report upon the subject of improving our judicial system. The act authorizing the appointment requires the Commission to report whether defects like those in our procedure have been successfully remedied elsewhere, and "if so, by what means."[1]

The Commission will find, upon investigation, that such defects have been successfully remedied in England, in her self-governing colonies, and in Connecticut; and that the remedy was effected by means of adopting and applying a few simple principles in their law of procedure. They are all embraced in this general and fundamental principle, *that the whole controversy be settled according to the substantive rights of the parties; completely; in one proceeding; by short and direct steps.*

This general principle subdivides into the following specific principles:

I. *The Principle of a Unified Jurisdiction.*—In England the power of administering justice in all civil cases, above the reach of county and local courts, is united in one jurisdiction and vested in one "Supreme Court," which is separated into distinct Divisions. For convenience, cases of law, equity, and probate are regularly assigned to the three respective Divisions of that court; but each Division has all the powers of the others. The Court of Appeal, which is the Appellate Division, has all the jurisdiction of the other Divisions for the purpose of finally determining the substantive rights of the parties on the appeal; and it may, in its discretion, admit new evidence, orally or by deposition—a power which, of course, is seldom used.[2] (Judicature Act [1873], secs. 3, 16, 19, 24.) We, on the contrary, maintain the principle of

---

[1] The act is chapter 88 of the Laws of 1905. Its provisions respecting the scope of the inquiry and report are in the exact language of the resolutions of the State Bar Association adopted at the annual meeting June, 1904, and published in the N. J. Law Journal in August, 1904, Vol. XXVII, p. 255; and Year Book of N. J. State Bar Ass'n (1904), p. 20.

[2] *Ante*, chap. VII.

divided jurisdiction. Sometimes it is mutually exclusive, sometimes concurrent, often overlapping. Instances are, law and equity, probate, discovery, mechanics' liens, title to land in the Circuit and Common Pleas. In the one system, no civil case can fail or be much delayed for want of power in the court to decide it completely; in the other, for want of that power, cases may, and do sometimes, fail, or require a second suit to settle an incidental question which could be conveniently settled in the first. Some thirty cases giving instances are stated in previous chapters.[3] The English system requires the court to administer in one and the same action all legal and equitable relief and remedies to which the parties are entitled. In this provision the English avoided a mistake of the American codes of procedure; for the latter attempted to "abolish the distinction between actions at law and suits in equity," while maintaining the distinctive methods of trial and distinctive remedies, such as injunction and specific performance. Moreover, the phrase in the codes was ill-chosen and gave a handle for hostile construction; for you can abolish a distinction only when you can abolish an idea.

II. *The Principle of Unified Procedure.*—Every action (except those begun by prerogative writs) is conducted in one and the same form, save the differences incidental to different modes of trial in law, equity, probate and admiralty cases. That is, they use "the single form of action." (Order 1.)[4] We maintain the principle of multiform procedure. Instances of the confusion in pleading and the delay on demurrer caused by this principle are given in "Corbin's Rules," (2d ed.), page 47. Try to enumerate the forms of action, legal and equitable, which we have, and the conditions which separate them. What defenses are allowed now, in our state, under the general issue, in covenant, debt, trespass, case, assumpsit, replevin, detinue? Note the consequence if you begin by petition, instead of bill, in equity (*Re* Miller, 58

---

[3] *Ante*, chap. III, IV.
[4] The references to "Orders" and "Rules" are to the English Rules of Court. They may be found in the "Annual Practice" of which new editions, with notes, are issued yearly. It is in the libraries of the New York Law Institute, and the New York City Bar Association. For a succinct and admirably clear exposition of the English procedure see W. B Odgers' "Procedure, Pleading and Practice" under the Judicature Acts (5th ed., London, 1903).

Atl. 383); or by supplemental, instead of by original, bill (Guild *v.* Meyer, 14 Dick. 390).[5]

III. *The Principle of Judicial Control over Procedure.*—The English statutes fix only the principles and outlines of their procedure; the details are regulated by rules of court. The Judicature Act of 1873 had only 100 sections, and most of these dealt with the organization of the court. There are about 1,200 Rules of Court, but they embrace a much wider range of subjects than we include in our procedure acts. The Connecticut Practice Act has only 34 sections, and the Rules of Court number 326.

In the English system nearly every step in the cause is under the discretionary control of the court. If you make a slip, your adversary has not the *right* to defeat or delay your action; but the court may suspend the rule as to your case on such terms as will guard him from surprise or loss, and penalize you, in costs, for your neglect. (Order 64, Rule 7; Order 70.) The procedure is flexible. Changes in the Rules are made from time to time by a "Rules Committee," consisting of members of the Bench and Bar. (Jud. Acts [1881], sec. 19, and [1894] sec. 4.) Here again the English avoided a mistake of the American Codes; for these, notably the present New York Code, carry statutory regulations into minute details.

With us, details of procedure are mostly set by fixed rules of statute and of common law. The court is bound by them, and either party has the right to invoke them to hinder the action. We adopt the principle of discretionary judicial control in the case of amendments and in some other instances, but to a very limited extent as compared with the English system.

In our state there are 937 sections in the following acts dealing specifically with procedure, and in the Rules of Court, viz.: In the (revised) Practice Act, Chancery Act, Courts Acts (L. 1900, pp. 343-362), and the (unrevised) Ejectment Act, Replevin Act; Rules of the Court of Appeals, of the Chancery, of the Supreme, of the Prerogative, and of the Orphans, courts. There are also many other statutes which regulate procedure, *e.g.,* Abatement, Attachment, Executions, Judgments, Lis Pendens, Orphans Courts, etc. Nearly every year some of these laws receive desultory amendments adding to their bulk.

---

[5] See the forms of action discussed in chap. VIII, *ante.*

In actual practice under the Judicature Acts, the application of the three principles above stated has eliminated from English litigation nearly every possible technical bar to a determination of the substantive rights of the parties in the pending case. Want of jurisdiction may, indeed, bar that determination; but less often than with us, because jurisdiction is unified. It cannot be barred by mistakes in choosing the form of action, because there is no choice; nor by slips in steps in the cause, because the court may excuse the slip. Questions of procedure arise constantly, but they never defeat the action or the appeal, save in the very rare cases where the court has no jurisdiction, or where the conduct of the party violating the rule of procedure is such that he has forfeited the right to be heard on the merits. A careful search in English reports and books of practice for cases defeated on points of procedure has convinced me of these practical achievements of the English reform.

IV. *The Principle of Completely Settling the Controversy in one Proceeding.*—The principle is applied not only by giving legal and equitable relief in the same action, but also by a wide extension of the right to join parties and causes of action in one proceeding.

(1) *Parties.*—The right to join as plaintiffs does not, as with us, hinge upon the technical point whether the right of action is joint or several, but upon the practical point whether the questions to be tried by the different plaintiffs are the same questions; arising from the same transactions and depending on the same evidence. The right to join parties as defendants is also much wider than with us. Any abuse of these rights is checked by the power of the court to strike out improper parties, to impose costs, and to order separate trials. The rules upon this point and the limits upon the right to join parties are stated under Order 16. No action can be defeated for misjoinder or nonjoinder. The remedy for such a mistake is by motion to add or strike out. (Order 16, Rule 11.) For illustrations of the difficulties raised by our law respecting parties, see a previous chapter in this book.[6]

(2) *Causes of Action.*—With a few exceptions, plaintiff may unite any causes of action, including tort and contract, subject to the discretionary

---

[6] Chap. IX. For a summary of the English rules on parties, see Odgers' "Principles of Pleading and Procedure."

power of the court to order separate trials, or to exclude causes of action which cannot be conveniently tried together. (Order 18.) Thus the right to settle two controversies, or two branches of one controversy, in one proceeding, depends, not, as with us, upon the technical question whether they are in tort or contract, but on the practical question of convenience. We adopt that principle in equity procedure (Ferry *v.* Laible, 12 C. E. G. 146).

(3) *Counterclaim.*—The defendant may make a counterclaim against plaintiff for any cause of action, in tort or contract, or arising from the same or a different transaction, subject to the same limitations of convenience and of control of the court as those which govern the plaintiff's right to join his causes of action.[7] (Order 19, Rule 3.)

(4) *Third Parties.*—Third parties, whose rights are involved in the controversy, may be brought in by the defendant. Thus, in a suit by a creditor against a surety, the latter may bring in, as a party, the principal debtor, and the court may control the action so that no party be required to wait unnecessarily upon the progress of the cause again another. (Jud. Act [1873], sec. 24, (3); Order 16, Rules 48-55.)

V. *The Principle that the Action Shall Proceed by Short and Direct Steps.*

(1) Every step means just what it purports to mean. There are no fictions. The summons commands the defendant to enter an appearance within a stated time, and warns him that, on his default, judgment will be entered against him. (Order 2, Rules 1-3.) The summons must be indorsed with a statement of the true nature of the claim and the true amount claimed, where it is known to plaintiff.

The pleadings must contain only a concise statement of the actual substantive facts (but not the evidence of those facts) to be proved. Facts cannot be pleaded according to legal effect. Neither party can prove what he does not state in his pleadings, except upon amendment, which is allowed in the discretion of the court. The court has unlimited power to allow amendments, upon terms.[8] (Orders 19, 28.)

---

[7] Chap. X, *ante.*
[8] Chap. XI, *ante.*

(2) Every step is a short and direct step to the given end. The following are instances:

Limiting the Defense.—In any action on contract for a specific sum, and in some other actions, if the defendant appears, he may, on plaintiff's application, be called on to satisfy the court (through its Master) that he has a *bona fide* defense. If it is sham, judgment goes against him immediately. If it is suspicious, terms may be imposed upon him, as to giving security, as to immediate trial, or the like. (Order 14.) About one-fourth of the total number of judgments entered yearly are entered under this practice. Our practice of striking out sham pleas is not nearly as efficacious to prevent the delays and subterfuges of pretended defenses.

No Demurrers.—There are no demurrers. Points of law may be raised in the answer, and are usually disposed of at the trial; but if they go to the merits of the whole case they may be heard previous to trial. (Order 25.) No time is lost over defective statements in the pleadings, which do not mislead; for the opposite party may demand particulars or a more definite pleading, or, on short notice, may have the defective statement amended or struck out upon the spot. (Order 19, Rule 7.)

Jury Finds Disputed Facts Specially.—The jury is usually required to find the disputed facts in issue, specific questions being submitted to them in writing, and judgment is entered for the party entitled, by the trial judge, upon those findings. (See an article by M. D. Chalmers, a judge of the English County Court, in 16 Am. Law Rev. [1822], pp. 873, 891.)

New Trials.—This practice must lessen the granting of new trials.[9] With us, verdicts being almost always general, new trials are granted on grounds which may have no relation to the facts on which the jury found its verdict. For instance, in ejectment, to try the validity of a will attacked on the grounds of illegal execution and undue influence, if a general verdict be given against the will, a new trial may be granted for rulings of the trial judge which relate to one of those grounds only, though the jury found its verdict entirely on the other ground; for the court cannot know on which ground the verdict was found.

---

[9] See the statement in chap. XV as to the number of new trials granted in England.

Moreover, by this practice, the facts in dispute being found by the jury, the court of review may, in a proper case, reverse the judgment and enter it for the party entitled to it, without a new trial. "Motions for judgment" in the English procedure mean applications of the latter kind. They are always made in the Court of Appeal and are, in fact, appeals from the judgment entered below by the trial judge upon the facts specially found by him or by the jury, as the case may be. (Order 40, Rules 3, 4.)

Appeals.—Our procedure on bills of exceptions does not exist in England. All appellate procedure is by appeal, and is in the nature of a rehearing. (Order 58.) It is taken upon a notice of appeal which states the points appealed from. The Court of Appeal may, in its discretion, take additional evidence orally or by deposition, and has all the jurisdiction of the Court below for the purpose of determining the appeal according to the substantive rights of the parties. It pronounces the judgment which the Court below ought to have pronounced.[10] (Order 58, Rule 4.)

Points of Procedure are Settled Summarily and Promptly.—If a question of procedure is one on which the final judgment must depend, it must be raised at the first opportunity before a judge, or it is waived. An appeal from his decision must be taken immediately, if at all. It goes directly to the Court of Appeal, and has preference there over appeals from final judgments.

Writs of Injunction and of Mandamus.—Orders or judgments of court are used in place of these writs. (Order 50, Rule 11; Order 53, Rule 4.)

There are other provisions for short and direct steps in expedition of the cause and for simplifying the proceedings. They are too many to enumerate here. Some of them are, the "Summons for Directions" (Order 30), "Discovery and Inspection" (Order 31), "Admissions" (Order 32), "Originating Summons" (Order 54A).

The five principles above stated were all adopted in the Connecticut Practice Act of 1879 and Rules of Court made by its authority. Those principles were not all carried to the same extent as in the English procedure, nor were they all embodied in the same methods, but to a sufficient extent and by sufficient methods to mark the judicial procedure of that state as closely

---

[10] See chap. XIII.

resembling the English in its essential features. It has proved satisfactory after twenty-four years' experience.[11]

Can we not adopt those principles in our procedure with advantage, limiting the extent and methods of their application as the conditions here may require?

---

[11] I have a letter from Judge Baldwin, of the Supreme Court of Errors of Connecticut, saying that "David Dudley Field said that our Connecticut system of reform procedure was the best anywhere, and I think that he is right." Judge Baldwin says that the act will probably be extended this year to the few excepted actions. He also says that there has been no practical difficulty found in giving effect to the provision requiring legal and equitable remedies to be administered in the same suit, and that he recollects no case in which a new trial has been ordered on the ground that a jury trial was erroneously refused by the court below in the mistaken view that the right involved was an equ1table, instead of a common-law, right.

APPENDIX.

(NOTE.—I regret that there is not space in this Appendix for the Connecticut Practice Act and Rules of Court. They are in much more concise language than the Judicature Acts and English Rules of Court.)

I.

SELECTIONS FROM THE ENGLISH JUDICATURE ACTS.

The title of the first Act is "THE SUPREME COURT OF JUDICATURE ACT, 1873." (36 & 37 VICT. CHAP. 66.)

Constitution and Judges of Supreme Court.

3. The several courts hereinafter mentioned (that is to say), the High Court of Chancery of England, the Court of Queen's Bench, the Court of Common Pleas at Westminster, the Court of Exchequer, the High Court of Admiralty, the Court of Probate, the Court for Divorce and Matrimonial Causes, and the London Court of Bankruptcy, shall be united and consolidated together, and shall constitute, under and subject to the provisions of this act, one Supreme Court of Judicature in England.

4. The said Supreme court shall consist of two permanent divisions, one of which, under the name of "Her Majesty's High Court of Justice," shall have and exercise original jurisdiction, with such appellate jurisdiction from inferior courts as is hereinafter mentioned, and the other of which, under the name of "Her Majesty's Court of Appeal," shall have and exercise appellate jurisdiction, with such original jurisdiction as hereinafter mentioned as may be incident to the determination of any appeal.

(Section 5 made the judges of the courts so consolidated judges of the High court.)

Jurisdiction and Law.

16. The High court shall be a superior court of record, and, subject as in this act mentioned, there shall be transferred to and vested in the High court the jurisdiction which, at the commencement of this act, was vested in, or capable of being exercised by, all or any of the courts following (that is to say):

(1) The High Court of Chancery, as a common-law court as well as a court of equity, including the jurisdiction of the Master of the Rolls, as a judge or master of the Court of Chancery, and any jurisdiction exercised by him in relation to the Court of Chancery as a common-law court;

(2) The Court of the Queen's Bench;

(3) The Court of Common Pleas at Westminster;

(4) The Court of Exchequer, as a court of revenue, as well as a common-law court;

(5) The High Court of Admiralty;

(6) The Court of Probate;

(7) The Court for Divorce and Matrimonial Causes;

(8) The London Court of Bankruptcy;

(9) The Court of Common Pleas at Lancaster;

(10) The Court of Pleas at Durham;

(11) The courts created by commissions of assize, of oyer and terminer, and of gaol delivery, or any of such commissions.

18. The Court of Appeal established by this act shall be a superior court of record, and there shall be transferred to and vested in such court all jurisdiction and powers of the courts following (that is to say):

(1) All jurisdiction and powers of the Lord Chancellor and of the Court of Appeal in Chancery, in the exercise of his and its appellate jurisdiction, and of the same court as a court of appeal in bankruptcy;

(2) All jurisdiction and powers of the Court of Appeal in Chancery of the county palatine of Lancaster, and all jurisdiction and powers of the Chancellor of the duchy and county palatine of Lancaster when sitting alone or apart from the Lords Justices of Appeal in Chancery as a judge of rehearing on appeal from decrees or orders of the Court of Chancery of the county palatine of Lancaster;

(3) All jurisdiction and powers of the Court of the Lord Warden of the Stannaries, assisted by his assessors, including all jurisdiction and powers of the said Lord Warden when sitting in his capacity of judge;

(4) All jurisdiction and powers of the Court of Exchequer Chamber;

(5) All jurisdiction vested in or capable of being exercised by Her Majesty in Council, or the Judicial Committee of Her Majesty's Privy Council, upon appeal from any judgment or order of the High Court of Admiralty, or from any order in lunacy made by the Lord Chancellor, or any other person having jurisdiction in lunacy.

19. The Court of Appeal shall have jurisdiction and power to hear and determine appeals from any judgment or order, save as hereinafter mentioned, of Her Majesty's High Court, or of any judges or judge thereof, subject to the provisions of this act, and to such rules and orders of court for regulating the terms and conditions on which such appeals shall be allowed, as may be made pursuant to this act.

For all the purposes of and incidental to the hearing and determination of any appeal within its jurisdiction, and the amendment, execution, and enforcement of any judgment or order made on any such appeal, and for the purpose of every other authority expressly given to the Court of Appeal by this act, the Court of Appeal shall have all the power, authority, and jurisdiction by this act vested in the High Court of Justice.

24. In every civil cause or matter commenced in the High court law and equity shall be administered by the High court and Court of Appeal respectively according to the rules following:

(1) If any plaintiff or petitioner claims to be entitled to any equitable estate or right, or to relief upon any equitable ground against any deed, instrument, or contract, or against any right, title, or claim whatsoever asserted by any defendant or respondent in such cause or matter, or to any relief founded upon a legal right, which heretofore could only have been given by a court of equity, the said courts respectively, and every judge thereof, shall give to such plaintiff or petitioner such and the same relief as ought to have been given by the Court of Chancery in a suit or proceeding for the same or the like purpose properly instituted before the passing of this act.

(2) If any defendant claims to be entitled to any equitable estate or right, or to relief upon any equitable ground against any deed, instrument, or

contract, or against any right, title, or claim asserted by any plaintiff or petitioner in such cause or matter, or alleges any ground of equitable defense to any claim of the plaintiff or petitioner in such cause or matter, the said courts respectively, and every judge thereof, shall give to every equitable estate, right, or ground of relief so claimed, and to every equitable defense so alleged, such and the same effect, by way of defense against the claim of such plaintiff or petitioner, as the Court of Chancery ought to have given if the same or the like matters had been relied on by way of defense in any suit or proceeding instituted in that court for the same or the like purpose before the passing of this act.

(3) The said courts, respectively, and every judge thereof, shall also have power to grant to any defendant in respect of any equitable estate or right, or other matter of equity, and also in respect of any legal estate, right, or title claimed or asserted by him, all such relief against any plaintiff or petitioner as such defendant shall have properly claimed by his pleading, and as the said courts respectively, or any judge thereof, might have granted in any suit instituted for that purpose by the same defendant against the same plaintiff or petitioner; and also all such relief relating to or connected with the original subject of the cause or matter, and in like manner claimed against any other person, whether already a party to the same cause or matter or not, who shall have been duly served with notice in writing of such claim, pursuant to any rule of court or any order of the court, as might properly have been granted against such person if he had been made a defendant to a cause duly instituted by the same defendant for the like purpose; and every person served with any such notice shall thenceforth be deemed a party to such cause or matter, with the same rights in respect of his defense against such claim, as if he had been duly sued in the ordinary way by such defendant.

(4) The said courts respectively, and every judge thereof, shall recognize and take notice of all equitable estates, titles, and rights, and all equitable duties and liabilities appearing incidentally in the course of any cause or matter, in the same manner in which the Court of Chancery would have recognized and taken notice of the same in any suit or proceeding duly instituted therein before the passing of this act.

(5) No cause or proceeding at any time pending in the High court or before the Court of Appeal, shall be restrained by prohibition or injunction; but

every matter of equity on which an injunction against the prosecution of any such cause or proceeding might have been obtained, if this act had not passed, either unconditionally or on any terms or conditions, may be relied on by way of defense thereto; provided always, that nothing in this act contained shall disable either of the said courts from directing a stay of proceedings in any cause or matter pending before it if it shall think fit; and any person, whether a party or not to any such cause or matter, who would have been entitled, if this act had not passed, to apply to any court to restrain the prosecution thereof, or who may be entitled to enforce, by attachment or otherwise, any judgment, decree, rule, or order, contrary to which all or any part of the proceedings in such cause or matter may have been taken, shall be at liberty to apply to the said courts respectively, by motion in a summary way, for a stay of proceedings in such cause or matter, either generally, or so far as may be necessary for the purposes of justice; and the court shall thereupon make such order as shall be just.

(6) Subject to the aforesaid provisions for giving effect to equitable rights and other matters of equity in manner aforesaid, and to the other express provisions of this act, the said courts respectively, and every judge thereof, shall recognize and give effect to all legal claims and demands, and all estates, titles, rights, duties, obligations, and liabilities existing by the common law or by any custom, or created by any statute, in the same manner as the same would have been recognized and given effect to if this act had not passed by any of the courts whose jurisdiction is hereby transferred to the High court.

(7) The High court and the Court of Appeal respectively, in the exercise of the jurisdiction vested in them by this act in every cause or matter pending before them respectively, shall have power to grant, and shall grant, either absolutely or on such reasonable terms and conditions as to them shall seem just, all such remedies whatsoever as any of the parties thereto may appear to be entitled to in respect of any and every legal or equitable claim properly brought forward by them respectively in such cause or matter; so that, as far as possible, all matters so in controversy between the said parties respectively, may be completely and finally determined, and all multiplicity of legal proceedings concerning any of such matters avoided.

(The eleventh subsection of section 25 is as follows):

(11) Generally, in all matters not hereinbefore particularly mentioned, in which there is any conflict or variance between the rules of equity and the rules of the common law with reference to the same matter, the rules of equity shall prevail.

(By section 31, the High court was divided into five divisions, namely, Chancery Division, Queen's Bench Division, Common Pleas Division, Exchequer Division, and Probate, Divorce and Admiralty Division. Section 32 authorized the Queen by Order in Council, to reduce the number of Divisions. By Order in Council (December 16, 1880), the Common Pleas and Exchequer Divisions were consolidated with the Queen's Bench Division.)

33. All causes and matters which may be commenced in, or which shall be transferred by this act to, the High court, shall be distributed among the several divisions and judges of the High court, in such manner as may from time to time be determined by any rules of court, or orders of transfer, to be made under the authority of this act; and in the meantime, and subject thereto, all such causes and matters shall be assigned to the said divisions respectively, in the manner herein after provided. Every document by which any cause or matter may be commenced in the High court shall be marked with the name of the division, or with the name of the judge, to which or to whom the same is assigned.

36. Any cause or matter may at any time, and at any stage thereof, and either with or without application from any of the parties thereto, be transferred by such authority and in such manner as rules of court may direct, from one division or judge of the High court to any other division or judge thereof, or may by the like authority be retained in the division in which the same was commenced, although such may not be the proper division to which the same cause or matter ought, in the first instance, to have been assigned.

(Section 40 provides for Divisional courts, but its provisions are amended by the JUDICATURE ACT OF 1876, section 17, which is as follows):

[17. Every action and proceeding in the High Court of Justice, and all business arising out of the same, except as is hereinafter provided, shall, so far as is practicable and convenient, be heard, determined, and disposed of before a single judge, and all proceedings in an action subsequent to the hearing or trial, and down to and including the final judgment or order, except as aforesaid, and always excepting any proceedings on appeal in the Court of

Appeal, Shall, so far as is practicable and convenient, be had and taken before the judge before whom the trial or hearing of the cause took place; Provided, nevertheless, that Divisional courts of the High Court of Justice may be held for the transaction of any business which may for the time being be ordered by rules of court to be heard by a Divisional court; and any such Divisional court when held shall be constituted of two judges of the court and no more, unless the president of the division to which such Divisional court belongs, with the concurrence of the other judges of such division, or a majority thereof, is of opinion that such Divisional court should be constituted of a greater number of judges than two, in which case such court may be constituted of such number of judges as the president, with such concurrence as aforesaid, may think expedient; nevertheless the decisions of a divisional court shall not be invalidated by reason of such court being constituted of a greater number than two judges; * * *.]

(The JUDICATURE ACT OF 1873 continues as follows):

45. All appeals from Petty or Quarter Sessions, from a County court, or from any other inferior court, which might before the passing of this act have been brought to any court or judge whose jurisdiction is by this act transferred to the High court, may be heard and determined by Divisional courts of the High court, consisting respectively of such of the judges thereof as may, from time to time, be assigned for that purpose, pursuant to the rules of court, or (subject to rules of court) as may be so assigned according to arrangements made for the purpose by the judges of the High court. The determination of such appeals respectively by such Divisional courts shall be final unless special leave to appeal from the same to the Court of Appeal shall be given by the Divisional court by which any such appeal from an inferior court shall have been heard.

The JUDICATURE ACT (1873) contained 100 sections.

Appeals.

(The JUDICATURE ACT (1873) contained no definition of appealable matters, and no express limitation upon the judgments or orders which might be appealed.)

Judicature Act (1875)

12. Every appeal to the Court of Appeal shall, where the subject-matter of the appeal is a final order, decree, or judgment, be heard before not less than three judges of the said court sitting together, and shall, when the subject-matter of the appeal is an interlocutory order, decree, or judgment, be heard before not less than two judges of the said court sitting together.

Any doubt which may arise as to what decrees, orders, or judgments are final, and what are interlocutory, shall be determined by the Court of Appeal.

Subject to the provisions contained in this section, the Court of Appeal may sit in two divisions at the same time.

(By the Judicature Act of 1902, the Court of Appeal was authorized to sit in three divisions. See chapter XIII, note 13.)

Judicature Act (1894).

1. (1) No appeal shall lie:
(a) From an order allowing an extension of time for appealing from a judgment or order; nor
(b) Without the leave of the judge, or of the Court of Appeal, from any interlocutory order or interlocutory judgment made or given by a judge, except in the following cases, namely:
(i) Where the liberty of the subject or the custody of infants is concerned; and
(ii) Cases of granting or refusing an injunction or appointing a receiver; and
(iii) Any decision determining the claim of any creditor or the liability of any contributory, or the liability of any director or other officer under the Companies Acts, 1862 to 1890, in respect of misfeasance or otherwise; and
(iv) Any decree *nisi* in a matrimonial cause, and any judgment or order in an admiralty action determining liability; and
(v) Any order on a special case stated under the Arbitration Act, 1889; and
(vi) Such other cases, to be prescribed by rules of court, as may, in the opinion of the authority for making such rules, be of the nature of final decisions.

(2) An order refusing unconditional leave to defend an action shall not be deemed to be an interlocutory order within the meaning of this section.

(3) No appeal shall lie from an order of a judge giving unconditional leave to defend an action.

(4) In matters of practice and procedure every appeal from a judge shall be to the Court of Appeal.

(5) In all cases where there is a right of appeal to the High court from any court or person, the appeal shall be heard and determined by a Divisional court constituted as may be prescribed by rules of court; and the determination thereof by the Divisional court shall be final, unless leave to appeal is given by that court or by the Court of Appeal.

(6) An application for leave to appeal may be made *ex parte* or otherwise, as may be prescribed by rules of court.

Statutory Power to Make Rules of Court.

(The power of making rules is regulated by the Judicature Act of 1873, and subsequent amendatory acts, as follows):

Judicature Act (1873).

75. A council of the judges of the Supreme court, of which due notice shall be given to all the said judges, shall assemble once at least in every year, on such day or days as shall be fixed by the Lord Chancellor, with the concurrence of the Lord Chief Justice of England, for the purpose of considering the operation of this act and of the rules of court for the time being in force, and also the working of the several offices and the arrangements relative to the duties of the officers of the said courts respectively, and of inquiring and examining into any defects which may appear to exist in the system of procedure or the administration of the law in the High court or the Court of Appeal, or in any other court from which any appeal lies to the High court or any judge thereof, or to the Court of Appeal; and they shall report annually to one of Her Majesty's principal secretaries of state what (if any) amendments or alterations it would in their judgment be expedient to make in this act, or otherwise relating to the administration of justice, and what other provisions

(if any) which cannot be carried into effect without the authority of Parliament it would be expedient to make for the better administration of justice. Any extraordinary council of the said judges may also at any time be convened by the Lord Chancellor.

(The Judicature Act of 1873 had rules of court appended to it. They had the effect of law. But the seventeenth section of the Judicature Act of 1875 authorized the Supreme court to make rules "for regulating the practice and procedure in the High Court and Court of Appeals;" and required all such rules to be laid before Parliament and (section 25) subject to be annulled by order in Council made upon an address to the crown from either house of Parliament. The twenty-fourth section of that act follows):

Judicature Act (1875).

24. Where any provisions in respect of the practice or procedure of any courts, the jurisdiction of which is transferred by the principal act or this act to the High court or the Court of Appeal, are contained in any act of Parliament, rules of court may be made for modifying such provisions to any extent that may be deemed necessary for adapting the same to the High court and the Court of Appeal.   *   *   *

Judicature Act (1881).

19. The power of making rules of court, conferred by section 17 of the Appellate Jurisdiction Act, 1876, upon the several judges therein mentioned, shall henceforth be vested in and exercised by any five or more of the following persons, of whom the Lord Chancellor shall be one; namely, the Lord Chancellor, the Lord Chief Justice of England, the Master of the Rolls, the President of the Probate, Divorce, and Admiralty Division of the High court, and four other judges of the Supreme court to be from time to time appointed for the purpose by the Lord Chancellor in writing under his hand, such appointment to continue for such time as shall be specified therein.

Judicature Act (1894).

3. It is hereby declared that the power to make rules conferred by the Judicature Acts, 1873 to 1891, includes power to make rules for regulating the means by which particular facts may be proved and the mode in which evidence thereof may be given.

4. The persons in whom the power of making rules of court pursuant to section 17 of the Appellate Jurisdiction Act, 1876, and section 19 of the Supreme Court of Judicature Act, 1881, is vested, shall include the president of the Incorporated Law Society for the time being, and shall also include two persons (one of whom shall be a practicing barrister) to be appointed for the purpose in the same manner as the four judges in the last-mentioned section referred to.

II.

SELECTIONS FROM THE RULES OF COURT.

The "Rules of the Supreme Court" of England are classified as "Orders" and "Rules." The Orders are merely names for divisions, or chapters of the rules. There are about 1,200 or 1,300 rules in all, dealing with a great variety of subjects. The following selections from them illustrate sufficiently the text of this book.

ORDER I.

Form and Commencement of Action.

1. All actions which previously to the commencement of the principal act, were commenced by writ in the superior courts of common law at Westminster, or in the Court of Common Pleas at Lancaster, or in the Court of Pleas at Durham, and all suits which, previously to the commencement of the principal act, were commenced by bill or information in the High Court of Chancery, or by a cause *in rem* or *in personam* in the High Court of Admiralty, or by citation or otherwise in the Court of Probate, shall be instituted in the High Court of Justice by a proceeding to be called an action.

ORDER II.

Writ of Summons and Procedure, Etc.

1. Every action in the High court shall be commenced by a writ of summons, which shall be indorsed with a statement of the nature of the claim made, or of the relief or remedy required in the action, and which shall specify the division of the High court to which it is intended that the action should be assigned.

3. The writ of summons for the commencement of an action shall, except in the cases in which any different form is hereinafter provided, be in one of

the Forms Nos. 1, 2, 3, and 4 in Appendix A, Part 1, with such variations as circumstances may require.

ORDER III.

Indorsement of Claim.

1. The indorsement of claim shall be made on every writ of summons before it is issued.

2. In the indorsement required by Order II, Rule 1, it shall not be essential to set forth the precise ground of complaint, or the precise remedy or relief to which the plaintiff considers himself entitled.

3. The indorsement of claim shall be to the effect of such of the forms in Appendix A, Part III, as shall be applicable to the case, or if none be found applicable, then such other similarly concise form as the nature of the case may require.

6. In all actions where the plaintiff seeks only to recover a debt or liquidated demand in money payable by the defendant, with or without interest, arising (a) upon a contract express or implied (as, for instance, on a bill of exchange, promissory note, or cheque, or other simple contract debt); or (b) on a bond or contract under seal for payment of a liquidated amount of money; or (c) on a statute where the sum sought to be recovered is a fixed sum of money or in the nature of a debt other than a penalty; or (d) on a guaranty, whether under seal or not, where the claim against the principal is in respect of a debt or liquidated demand only; or (e) on a trust; or (f) in actions for the recovery of land, with or without a claim for rent or mesne profits, by landlord against a tenant whose term has expired or has been duly determined by notice to quit, or against persons claiming under such tenant; the writ of summons may, at the option of the plaintiff, be specially indorsed with a statement of his claim, or of the remedy or relief to which he claims to be entitled. Such special indorsement shall be to the effect of such of the forms in Appendix C, Secs. I, V, as shall be applicable to the case.

7. Wherever the plaintiff's claim is for a debt or liquidated demand only, the indorsement, besides stating the nature of the claim, shall state the amount claimed for debt, or in respect of such demand, and for costs respectively, and

shall further state that upon payment thereof within four days after service, or in case of a writ not for service within the jurisdiction, within the time allowed for appearance, further proceedings will be stayed. Such statement shall be in the form in Appendix A, Part III, Sec. III.   * * *

(The defendant must enter an appearance to the summons either in person or by solicitor, if he wishes to defend (Order XII, Rule 8); and if he do not, judgment by default may be entered against him if the claim is for a liquidated sum.) (Order XIII, Rule 3; Order XXVII, Rule 2.)

ORDER XIV.

Leave to Sign Judgment and Defend Where Writ Specially Endorsed.

1. (a) Where the defendant appears to a writ of summons specially indorsed under Order III, Rule 6, the plaintiff may, on affidavit made by himself, or by any other person who can swear positively to the facts, verifying the cause of action, and the amount claimed (if any), and stating that in his belief there is no defense to the action, apply to a judge for liberty to enter final judgment for the amount so indorsed, together with interest, if any, or for recovery of the land (with or without rent or mesne profits), as the case may be, and costs. The judge may thereupon, unless the defendant by affidavit, by his own *viva voce* evidence, or otherwise, shall satisfy him that he has a good defense to the action on the merits, or disclose such facts as may be deemed sufficient to entitle him to defend, make an order empowering the plaintiff to enter judgment accordingly.

6. Leave to defend may be given unconditionally, or subject to such terms as to giving security or time or mode of trial or otherwise as the judge may think fit.

ORDER XVI.

Parties.

1. *Generally.*

1. All persons may be joined in one action as plaintiffs, in whom any right to relief in respect of or arising out of the same transaction or series of transactions is alleged to exist, whether jointly, severally, or in the alternative, where, if such persons brought separate actions, any common question of law or fact would arise; provided that, if, upon the application of any defendant, it shall appear that such joinder may embarrass or delay the trial of the action, the court or a judge may order separate trials, or make such other order as may be expedient, and judgment may be given for such one or more of the plaintiffs as may be found to be entitled to relief, for such relief as he or they may be entitled to, without any amendment. But the defendant, though unsuccessful, shall be entitled to his costs occasioned by so joining any person who shall not be found entitled to relief unless the court or a judge in disposing of the costs shall otherwise direct.

2. Where an action has been commenced in the name of the wrong person as plaintiff, or where it is doubtful whether it has been commenced in the name of the right plaintiff, the court or a judge may, if satisfied that it has been so commenced through a *bona fide* mistake, and that it is necessary for the determination of the real matter in dispute so to do, order any other person to be substituted or added as plaintiff upon such terms as may be just.

4. All persons may be joined as defendants against whom the right to any relief is alleged to exist, whether jointly, severally, or in the alternative. And judgment may be given against such one or more of the defendants as may be found to be liable, according to their respective liabilities, without any amendment.

5. It shall not be necessary that every defendant shall be interested as to all the relief prayed for, or as to every cause of action included in any proceeding against him; but the court or a judge may make such order as may appear just to prevent any defendant from being embarrassed or put to expense by being required to attend any proceedings in which he may have no interest.

6. The plaintiff may, at his option, join as parties to the same action all or any of the persons severally, or jointly and severally liable on any one contract, including parties to bills of exchange and promissory notes.

7. Where the plaintiff is in doubt as to the person from whom he is entitled to redress, he may, in such manner as hereinafter mentioned, or as may be prescribed by any special order, join two, or more defendants, to the intent that the question as to which, if any, of the defendants is liable, and to what extent, may be determined as between all parties.

8. Trustees, executors, and administrators may sue and be sued on behalf of or as representing the property or estate of which they are trustees or representatives, without joining any of the persons beneficially interested in the trust or estate, and shall be considered as representing such persons; but the court or a judge may, at any stage of the proceedings, order any of such persons to be made parties, either in addition to or in lieu of the previously existing parties.

This rule shall apply to trustees, executors and administrators, sued in proceedings to enforce a security by foreclosure or otherwise.

9. Where there are numerous persons having the same interest in one cause or matter, one or more of such persons may sue or be sued, or may be authorized by the court or a judge to defend in such cause or matter, on behalf or for the benefit of all persons so interested.

11. No cause or matter shall be defeated by reason of the misjoinder or nonjoinder of parties, and the court may in every cause or matter deal with the matter in controversy so far as regards the rights and interests of the parties actually before it. The court or a judge may, at any stage of the proceedings, either upon or without the application of either party, and on such terms as may appear to the court or a judge to be just, order that the names of any parties improperly joined, whether as plaintiffs or as defendants, be struck out, and that the names of any parties, whether plaintiffs or defendants, who ought to have been joined, or whose presence before the court may be necessary in order to enable the court effectually and completely to adjudicate upon and settle all the questions involved in the cause or matter, be added. No person shall be added as a plaintiff suing without a next friend, or as the next friend of a plaintiff under any disability, without his own consent in writing thereto. Every party whose name is so added as defendant shall be served with

a writ of summons or notice in manner hereinafter mentioned or in such manner as may be prescribed by any special order, and the proceedings as against such party shall be deemed to have begun only on the service of such writ or notice.

Third Party Procedure.

48. Where a defendant claims to be entitled to contribution, or indemnity over against any person not a party to the action, he may, by leave of the court or a judge, issue a notice (hereinafter called the third-party notice) to that effect, stamped with the seal with which writs of summons are sealed. A copy of such notice shall be filed with the proper officer and served on such person according to the rules relating to the service of writs of summons. The notice shall state the nature and grounds of the claim, and shall, unless otherwise ordered by the court or a judge, be served within the time limited for delivering his defense. Such notice may be in the form or to the effect of the Form No. 1 in Appendix B, with such variations as circumstances may require, and therewith shall be served a copy of the statement of claim, then a copy of the writ of summons in the action.

ORDER XVIII.

Joinder of Causes of Action.

1. Subject to the following rules of this order, the plaintiff may unite in the same action several causes of action; but if it appear to the court or a judge that any such causes of action cannot be conveniently tried or disposed of together, the court or judge may order separate trials of any of such causes of action to be had, or may make such other order as may be necessary or expedient for the separate disposal thereof.
2. No cause of action shall, unless by leave of the court or a judge, be joined with an action for the recovery of land, except claims in respect of mesne profits or arrears of rent or double value in respect of the premises claimed, or any part thereof, and damages for breach of any contract under which the

same or any part thereof are held, or for wrong or injury to the premises claimed. * * *

3. Claims by a trustee in bankruptcy as such shall not, unless by leave of the court or a judge, be joined with any claim by him in any other capacity.

4. Claims by or against husband and wife may be joined with claims by or against either of them separately.

5. Claims by or against an executor or administrator as such may be joined with claims by or against him personally, provided the last-mentioned claims are alleged to arise with reference to the estate in respect of which the plaintiff or defendant sues or is sued as executor or administrator.

6. Claims by plaintiffs jointly may be joined with claims by them or any or them separately against the same defendant.

7. The last three preceding rules shall be subject to Rules 1, 8, and 9 of this order.

8. Any defendant alleging that the plaintiff has united in the same action several causes of action which cannot be conveniently disposed of together, may at any time apply to the court or a judge for an order confining the action to such of the causes of action as may be conveniently disposed of together.

9. If, on the hearing of such application as in the last preceding rule mentioned, it shall appear to the court or a judge that the causes of action are such as cannot all be conveniently disposed of together, the court or judge may order any of such causes of action to be excluded, and consequential amendments to be made, and may make such order as to costs as may be just.

ORDER XVIIIa.

Trial Without Pleadings.

(If plaintiff wishes to proceed to trial without pleadings, he may proceed under this order as follows:)

1. The indorsement of the writ of summons shall contain a statement sufficient to give notice of the nature of his claim or of the relief or remedy required in the action, and shall state that if the defendant appears the plaintiff intends to proceed to trial without pleadings.

2. Within ten days after appearance the plaintiff shall serve twenty-one days' notice of trial without pleadings. Such notice shall be in Form No. 16(a), Appendix B, with such variations as circumstances may require.

3. The defendant may within ten days after appearance apply by summons for the delivery of a statement of claim, and on such summons the judge may order (1) that a statement of claim shall be delivered, in which case the action shall proceed in the usual manner; or (2) that the action shall proceed to trial without pleadings, in which case it may be further ordered, if the judge shall think fit, that either party shall deliver particulars of his claim or defense.

4. When the judge orders that the action shall proceed to trial without pleadings, and makes no order as to particulars, all defenses shall be open at the trial to the defendant. Where particulars are ordered to be delivered the parties shall be bound by such particulars, so far as regards the matters in respect of which the order for particulars was made.

ORDER XIX.

Pleading Generally.

1. The following rules of pleading shall be used in the High Court of Justice.

2. The plaintiff shall, subject to the provisions of Order XX, and at such time and in such manner as therein prescribed, deliver to the defendant a statement of his claim, and of the relief or remedy to which he claims to be entitled. The defendant shall, subject to the provisions of Order XXI, and at such time and in such manner as therein prescribed, deliver to the plaintiff his defense, set-off, or counterclaim (if any), and the plaintiff shall, subject to the provisions of Order XXIII, and at such time and in such manner as therein prescribed, deliver his reply (if any) to such defense, set-off, or counterclaim. Such statements shall be as brief as the nature of the case will admit, and the taxing officer in adjusting the costs of the action shall at the instance of any party, or may without any request, inquire into any unnecessary prolixity, and order the costs occasioned by such prolixity to be borne by the party chargeable with the same.

3. A defendant in an action may set-off, or set up by way of counterclaim against the claims of the plaintiff, any right or claim, whether such set-off or counterclaim sound in damages or not, and such set-off or counterclaim shall have the same effect as a cross-action, so as to enable the court to pronounce a final judgment in the same action, both on the original and on the cross-claim. But the court or a judge may, on the application of the plaintiff before trial, if in the opinion of the court or judge such set-off or counterclaim cannot be conveniently disposed of in the pending action, or ought not to be allowed, refuse permission to the defendant to avail himself thereof.

4. Every pleading shall contain, and contain only, a statement in a summary form of the material facts on which the party pleading relies for his claim or defense, as the case may be, but not the evidence by which they are to be proved, and shall, when necessary, be divided into paragraphs, numbered consecutively; dates, sums, and numbers shall be expressed in figures and not in words; signature of counsel shall not be necessary; but where pleadings have been settled by counsel or a special pleader they shall be signed by him; and if not so settled they shall be signed by the solicitor, or by the party if he sues or defends in person.

5. The forms in Appendices C, D, and E, when applicable, and where they are not applicable, forms of the like character, as near as may be, shall be used for all pleadings, and where such forms are applicable and sufficient any longer forms shall be deemed prolix, and the costs occasioned by such prolixity shall be disallowed to or borne by the party so using the same, as the case may be.

7. A further and better statement of the nature of the claim or defense, or further and better particulars of any matter stated in any pleading, notice, or written proceeding requiring particulars, may in all cases be ordered, upon such terms as to costs and otherwise, as may be just.

13. Every allegation of fact in any pleading, not being a petition or summons, if not denied specially or by necessary implication, or stated to be not admitted in the pleading of the opposite party, shall be taken to be admitted, except as against an infant, lunatic, or person of unsound mind not so found by inquisition.

15. The defendant or plaintiff (as the case may be) must raise by his pleading all matters which show the action or counterclaim not to be maintainable, or that the transaction is either void or voidable in point of law,

and all such grounds of defense or reply, as the case may be, as if not raised, would be likely to take the opposite party by surprise, or would raise issues of fact not arising out of the preceding pleadings, as, for instance, fraud, Statute of Limitations, release, payment, performance, facts, showing illegality either by statute or common law, or Statute of Frauds.

17. It shall not be sufficient for a defendant in his statement of defense to deny generally the grounds alleged by the statement of claim, or for a plaintiff in his reply to deny generally the grounds alleged in a defense by way of counter-claim, but each party must deal specifically with each allegation of fact of which he does not admit the truth, except damages.

18. Subject to the last preceding rule, the plaintiff by his reply may join issue upon the defense, and each party in his pleading (if any) subsequent to reply, may join issue upon the previous pleading. Such joinder of issue shall operate as a denial of every material allegation of fact in the pleading upon which issue is joined, but it may except any facts which the party may be willing to admit, and shall then operate as a denial of the facts not so admitted.

19. When a party in any pleading denies an allegation of fact in the previous pleading of the opposite party, he must not do so evasively, but answer the point of substance. Thus, if it be alleged that he received a certain sum of money, it shall not be sufficient to deny that he received that particular amount, but he must deny that he received that sum or any part thereof, or else set out how much he received. And if an allegation is made with divers circumstances, it shall not be sufficient to deny it along with those circumstances.

20. When a contract, promise, or agreement is alleged in any pleading, a bare denial of the same by the opposite party shall be construed only as a denial in fact of the express contract, promise, or agreement alleged, or of the matters of fact from which the same may be implied by law, and not as a denial of the legality or sufficiency in law of such contract, promise, or agreement, whether with reference to the Statute of Frauds or otherwise.

26. No technical objection shall be raised to any pleading on the ground of any alleged want of form.

27. The court or a judge may at any stage of the proceedings order to be struck out or amended any matter in any indorsement or pleading which may be unnecessary or scandalous or which may tend to prejudice, embarrass, or delay the fair trial of the action; and may in any such case, if they or he shall

think fit, order the costs of the application to be paid as between solicitor and client.

(ORDER XX regulates the "Statement of Claim," which is the plaintiff's first pleading. None is used if the summons has been "specially indorsed" under Order III. If defendant appears, no statement of claim need be served or filed, in general, unless demanded by him or ordered by the court or a master under Order XXX.)

6. Every statement of claim shall state specifically the relief which the plaintiff claims, either simply or in the alternative, and it shall not be necessary to ask for general or other relief, which may always be given, as the court or a judge may think just, to the same extent as if it had been asked for. And the same rule shall apply to any counterclaim made, or relief claimed by the defendant, in his defense.

ORDER XXI.

Defense and Counterclaim.

1. In actions for a debt or liquidated demand in money comprised in Order III, Rule 6, a mere denial of the debt shall be inadmissible.

2. In actions upon bills of exchange, promissory notes, or cheques, a defense in denial must deny some matter of fact; *e.g.*, the drawing, making, indorsing, accepting, presenting, or notice of dishonor of the bill or note.

3. In actions comprised in Order III, Rule 6, classes (a) and (b), a defense in denial must deny such matters of fact, from which the liability of the defendant is alleged to arise, as are disputed; *e.g.*, in actions for goods bargained and sold or sold and delivered, the defense must deny the order or contract, the delivery or the amount claimed; in an action for money had and received, it must deny the receipt of the money, or the existence of those facts which are alleged to make such receipt by the defendant a receipt to the use of the plaintiff.

4. No denial or defense shall be necessary as to damages claimed or their amount; but they shall be deemed to be put in issue in all cases, unless expressly admitted.

5. If either party wishes to deny the right of any other party to claim as executor, or as trustee whether in bankruptcy or otherwise, or in any

representative or other alleged capacity, or the alleged constitution of any partnership firm, he shall deny the same specifically.

6. Where a statement of claim is delivered to a defendant he shall deliver his defense within ten days from the delivery of the statement of claim, or from the time limited for appearance, whichever shall be last, unless such time is extended by the court or judge.

9. Where the court or a judge shall be of opinion that any allegation of fact denied or not admitted by the defense ought to have been admitted, the court or judge may make, such order as shall be just with respect to any extra costs occasioned by their having been denied or not admitted.

(Under Rules 11-13, defendant may counter-claim against plaintiffs and third persons and bring in such third persons as parties.)

17. Where in any action a set-off or counter-claim is established as a defense against the plaintiff's claim, the court or a judge may, if the balance is in favor of the defendant, give judgment for the defendant for such balance, or may otherwise adjudge to the defendant such relief as he may be entitled to upon the merits of the case.

20. No plea or defense shall be pleaded in abatement.

21. No defendant in an action for the recovery of land who is in possession by himself or his tenant need plead his title, unless his defense depends on an equitable estate or right or he claims relief upon any equitable ground against any right or title asserted by the plaintiff. But, except in the cases hereinbefore mentioned, it shall be sufficient to state by way of defense that he is so in possession, and it shall be taken to be implied in such statement that he denies, or does not admit the allegations of fact contained in the plaintiff's statement of claim. He may nevertheless rely upon any ground of defense which he can prove except as hereinbefore mentioned.

ORDER XXIII.

Reply and Subsequent Pleadings.

1. A plaintiff shall deliver his reply, if any, in admiralty actions within six days, and in other actions within twenty-one days, after the defense or the last

of the defenses shall have been delivered, unless the time shall be extended by the court or a judge.

2. No pleading subsequent to reply other than a joinder of issue shall be pleaded without leave of the court or a judge, and then shall be pleaded only upon such terms as the court or judge shall think fit.

ORDER XXIV.

Matters Arising Pending the Actions.

1. Any ground of defense which has arisen after action brought, but before the defendant has delivered his statement of defense, and before the time limited for his doing so has expired, may be raised by the defendant in his statement of defense, either alone or together with other grounds of defense. And if, after a statement of defense has been delivered, any ground of defense arises to any set-off or counterclaim alleged therein by the defendant, it may be raised by the plaintiff in his reply, either alone or together with any other ground of reply.

2. Where any ground of defense arises after the defendant has delivered a statement of defense, or after the time limited for his doing so has expired, the defendant may, and where any ground of defense to any set-off or counterclaim arises after reply, or after the time limited for delivering a reply has expired, the plaintiff may, within eight days after such ground of defense has arisen, or at any subsequent time, by leave of the court, or a judge, deliver a further defense or further reply, as the case may be, setting forth the same.

ORDER XXV.

Proceedings in Lieu of Demurrer.

1. No demurrer shall be allowed.
2. Any party shall be entitled to raise by his pleading any point of law, and any point so raised shall be disposed of by the judge who tries the cause or after the trial, provided that by consent of the parties, or by order of the court or a

judge on the application of either party, the same may be set down for hearing and disposed of at any time before the trial.

3. If, in the opinion of the court or a judge, the decision of such point of law substantially disposes of the whole action, or of any distinct cause of action, ground of defense, set-off, counterclaim, or reply therein, the court or judge may thereupon dismiss the action or make such other order therein as may be just.

4. The court or a judge may order any pleading to be struck out, on the ground that it discloses no reasonable cause of action or answer, and in any such case or in case of the action or, defense being shown by the pleadings to be frivolous or vexatious, the court or a judge may order the action to be stayed or dismissed, or judgment to be entered accordingly, as may be just.

5. No action or proceeding shall be open to objection, on the ground that a merely declaratory judgment or order is sought thereby, and the court may make binding declarations of right whether any consequential relief is or could be claimed, or not.

ORDER XXVIII.

Amendment.

1. The court or a judge may, at any stage of the proceedings, allow either party to alter or amend his indorsement or pleadings, in such manner and on such terms as may be just, and all such amendments shall be made as may be necessary for the purpose of determining the real questions in controversy between the parties.

6. In all cases not provided for by the preceding rules of this order, application for leave to amend may be made by either party to the court or a judge, or to the judge at the trial of the action, and such amendment may be allowed upon such terms as to costs or otherwise as may be just.

11. Clerical mistakes in judgment or orders, or errors arising therein from any accidental slip or omission, may at any time be corrected by the court or a judge on motion or summons without an appeal.

12. The court or a judge may at any time, and on such terms as to costs or otherwise as the court or judge may think just, amend any defect or error in

any proceedings, and all necessary amendments shall be made for the purpose of determining the real question or issue raised by or depending on the proceedings.

ORDER XXX.

Summons for Directions.

1. (a) Subject as hereinafter mentioned, in every action a summons for directions shall be taken out by the plaintiff returnable in not less than four days.

(b) Such summons shall be taken out after appearance and before the plaintiff takes any fresh step in the action other than application for an injunction, or for a receiver, or for summary judgment under Order XIV, or to enter judgment in default of defense under Order XXVII, Rule 2.

(c) The summons shall be in the Form No. 3a, Appendix K, with such variations as circumstances may require, and shall be addressed to and served upon all such parties to the action as may be affected thereby.

2. Upon the hearing of the summons the court or a judge shall, so far as practicable, make such order as may be just with respect to all the interlocutory proceedings to be taken in the action before the trial, and as to the costs thereof, and more particularly with respect to the following matters: Pleading, particulars, admissions, discovery, interrogatories, inspection of documents, inspection of real or personal property, commissions, examination of witnesses, place and mode of trial. Such order shall be in the Form No. 4a, Appendix K, with such variations as circumstances may require.

6. Any application by any party which might have been made at the hearing of the original summons shall, if granted on any subsequent application, be granted at the costs of the party applying unless the court or a judge shall be of opinion that the application could not properly have been made at the hearing of the original summons.

7. On the hearing of the summons, the court or a judge may order that evidence of any particular fact, to be specified in the order, shall be given by statement on oath of information and belief, or by production of documents

or entries in books, or by copies of documents or entries or otherwise as the court or judge may direct.

(By a later rule all the proceedings under this order are taken before a master of the court, who makes the order under Rule 2, subject to appeal to a judge.)

(ORDER XXXI regulates discovery and inspection under its rules; interrogatories may be served by either party upon the other, by leave of a judge or a master.)

12. Any party may, without filing an affidavit, apply to the court or a judge for an order directing any other party to any cause or matter to make discovery on oath of the documents which are or have been in his possession or power, relating to any matter in question therein. On the hearing of such application the court or judge may either refuse or adjourn the same, if satisfied that such discovery is not necessary, or not necessary at that stage of the cause or matter, or make such order, either generally or limited to certain classes of documents, as may, in their or his discretion, be thought fit. Provided, that discovery shall not be ordered when and so far as the court or judge shall be of opinion that it is not necessary, either for disposing of the cause or matter or for saving costs.

14. It shall be lawful for the court or a judge, at any time during the pendency of any cause or matter, to order the production by any party thereto, upon oath, of such of the documents in his possession or power, relating to any matter in question in such cause or matter, as the court or judge shall think right; and the court may deal with such documents, when produced, in such manner as shall appear just.

(There are a number of rules under this order regulating the inspection of documents, and the control of the court over the subject is considerably wider than it is with us.)

ORDER XXXII.

Admissions.

1. Any party to a cause or matter may give notice, by his pleading, or otherwise in writing, that he admits the truth of the whole or any part of the case of any other party.

4. Any party may, by notice in writing, at any time not later than nine days before the day for which notice of trial has been given, call on any other party to admit, for the purposes of the cause, matter, or issue only, any specific fact or facts mentioned in such notice. And in case of refusal or neglect to admit the same within six days after service of such notice, or within such further time as may be allowed by the court or a judge, the costs of proving such fact or facts shall be paid by the party so neglecting or refusing, whatever the result of the cause, matter, or issue may be, unless at the trial or hearing the court or a judge certify that the refusal to admit was reasonable, or unless the court or a judge shall at any time otherwise order or direct. Provided, that any admission made in pursuance of such notice is to be deemed to be made only for the purposes of the particular cause, matter, or issue, and not as an admission to be used against the party on any other occasion or in favor of any person other than the party giving the notice; provided also, that the court or a judge may at any time allow any party to amend or withdraw any admission so made on such terms as may be just.

6. Any party may at any stage of a cause or matter, where admissions of fact have been made, either on the pleadings, or otherwise, apply to the court or a judge for such judgment or order as upon such admission he may be entitled to, without waiting for the determination of any other question between the parties; and the court or a judge may upon such application make such order, or give such judgment, as the court or judge may think just.

ORDER XXXIII.

Issues, Inquiries, and Accounts.

1. Where in any cause or matter it appears to the court or a judge that the issues of fact in dispute are not sufficiently defined, the parties may be directed to prepare issues, and such issues shall, if the parties differ, be settled by the court or a judge.

(ORDER XXXVI regulates trials. The right to jury trial in common-law cases is preserved by the Judicature Acts. It is waived, however, if not demanded.)

7. (a.) In every cause or matter, unless under the provisions of Rule 6 of this order a trial with a jury is ordered, or under Rule 2 of this order either party has signified a desire to have a trial with a jury, the mode of trial shall be by a judge without a jury; provided, that in any such case the court or a judge may at any time order any cause, matter, or issue to be tried by a judge with a jury, or by a judge sitting with assessors, or by an official referee or special referee with or without assessors.

8. Subject to the provisions of the preceding rules of this order, the court or a judge may, in any cause or matter, at any time or from time to time, order that different questions of fact arising therein be tried by different modes of trial, or that one or more questions of fact be tried before the others, and may appoint the places for such trials, and in all cases may order that one or more issues of fact be tried before any other or others.

39. The judge shall, at or after trial, direct judgment to be entered as he shall think right, and no motion for judgment shall be necessary in order to obtain such judgment.

ORDER XXXVII.

Evidence Generally.

1. In the absence of any agreement in writing between the solicitors of all parties, and subject to these rules, the witnesses at the trial of any action or at any assessment of damages shall be examined *viva voce* and in open court; but the court or a judge may at any time for sufficient reason order that any particular fact or facts may be proved by affidavit, or that the affidavit of any witness may be read at the hearing or trial, on such conditions as the court or judge may think reasonable, or that any witness whose attendance in court ought for some sufficient cause to be dispensed with be examined by interrogatories or otherwise before a commissioner or examiner; provided, that where it appears to the court or judge that the other party *bona fide* desires the production of a witness for cross-examination, and that such witness can be produced, an order shall not be made authorizing the evidence of such witness to be given by affidavit.

5. The court or a judge may, in any cause or matter where it shall appear necessary for the purposes of justice, make any order for the examination upon oath before the court or judge or any officer of the court, or any other person, and at any place, of any witness or person, and may empower any party to any such cause or matter to give such deposition in evidence therein on such terms, if any, as the court or a judge may direct.

ORDER XXXIX.

Motion for New Trial.

1. Every motion for a new trial or to set aside a verdict, finding, or judgment, shall be made, where there has been a trial without a jury, by appeal to the Court of Appeal. And upon the hearing of such motion the Court of Appeal shall have all such powers as are exercisable by it upon the hearing of an appeal.
2. No judge shall sit on the hearing of any motion for a new trial in any cause or matter tried with a jury before himself.
3. Every application for a new trial shall be by notice of motion, and no rule *nisi*, order to show cause, or formal proceeding other than such notice of motion, shall be made or taken. The notice shall state the grounds of the application, and whether all or part only of the verdict or findings is complained of.

(The notice of the motion is a fourteen days' notice.)

ORDER XL.

3. Where, at or after a trial with a jury, the judge has directed that any judgment be entered, any party may apply to set aside such judgment and enter any other judgment, on the ground that the judgment directed to be entered is wrong by reason that the finding of the jury upon the questions submitted to them has not been properly entered.
4. Where, at or after a trial by a judge, either with or without a jury, the judge has directed that any judgment be entered, any party may apply to set aside such judgment and to enter any other judgment, upon the ground that, upon, the finding as entered, the judgment so directed is wrong.

5. An application under Rules 3 and 4 of this order shall be to the Court of Appeal.

10. Upon a motion for judgment, or upon an application for a new trial, the court may draw all inferences of fact, not inconsistent with the finding of the jury, and if satisfied that it has before it all the materials necessary for finally determining the questions in dispute, or any of them, or for awarding any relief sought, give judgment accordingly, or may, if it shall be of opinion that it has not sufficient materials before it to enable it to give judgment, direct the motion to stand over for further consideration, and direct such issues or questions to be tried or determined, and such accounts and inquiries to be taken and made, as it may think fit.

ORDER XLIX.

Transfers and Consolidation.

1. Causes or matters may be transferred from one division to another of the High court or from one judge to another of the chancery division by an order of the Lord Chancellor, provided that no transfer shall be made from or to any division without the consent of the president of the division.

3. Any cause or matter may, at any stage, be transferred from one division to another by an order made by the court or any judge of the division to which the cause or matter is assigned; Provided, that no such transfer shall be made without the consent of the president of the division to which the cause or matter is proposed to be transferred.

ORDER LIII.

Action of Mandamus.

1. The plaintiff, in any action in which he shall claim a mandamus to command the defendant to fulfill any duty in the fulfillment of which the plaintiff is personally interested, shall indorse such claim upon the writ of summons.

3. If judgment be given for the plaintiff the court or judge may, by the judgment, command the defendant either forthwith, or on the expiration of such time and upon such terms as may appear to the court or a judge to be just, to perform the duty in question. The court or a judge may also extend the time for the performance of the duty.

4. No writ of mandamus shall hereafter be issued in an action, but a mandamus shall be by judgment or order, which shall have the same effect as a writ of mandamus formerly had.

ORDER LIV.

Appeals from Decisions of a Master; or a Judge at Chambers.

21. Any person affected by any order or decision of a master may appeal therefrom to a judge at chambers. Such appeal shall be by the way of indorsement on the summons by the master at the request of any party, or by notice in writing to attend before the judge without a fresh summons, within four days after the decision complained of, or such further as may be allowed by a judge or master.

23. In the Queen's Bench Division, except in matters of practice and procedure, the appeal from a decision of a judge at chambers shall be to a Divisional court.

24. In the Queen's Bench Division, except in matters of practice and procedure, every appeal to the court from any decision at chambers shall be by motion, and shall be made within eight days after the decision appealed against, or, if no court to which such appeal can be made shall sit within such eight days, then on the first day on which any such court may be sitting after the expiration of such eight days.

ORDER LIV-A.

Declaration on Originating Summons.

1. In any division of the High court, any person claiming to be interested under a deed, will, or other written instrument, may apply by originating

summons for the determination of any question of construction arising under the instrument, and for a declaration of the rights of the persons interested.

2. The court or a judge may direct such persons to be served with the summons as they or he may think fit.

3. The application shall be supported by such evidence as the court or a judge may require.

4. The court or judge shall not be bound to determine any such question of construction if in their or his opinion it ought not to be determined on originating summons.

(The proceedings upon originating summons are summary and expeditious. They are much used by trustees, executors, and in like cases.)

ORDER LVIII.

Appeals to the Court of Appeal.

1. All appeals to the Court of Appeal shall be by way of rehearing, and shall be brought by notice of motion in a summary way, and no petition, case, or other formal proceeding other than such notice of motion shall be necessary. The appellant may, by the notice of motion, appeal from the whole or any part of any judgment or order, and the notice of motion shall state whether the whole or part only of such judgment or order is complained of, and in the latter case shall specify such part.

2. The notice of appeal shall be served upon all parties directly affected by the appeal, and it shall not be necessary to serve parties not so affected; but the Court of Appeal may direct notice of the appeal to be served on all or any parties to the action or other proceeding, or upon any person not a party, and in the meantime may postpone or adjourn the hearing of the appeal upon such terms as may be just, and may give such judgment and make such order as might have been given or made if the persons served with such notice had been originally parties. Any notice of appeal may be amended at any time as the Court of Appeal may think fit.

3. Notice of appeal from any judgment, whether final or interlocutory, or from a final order, shall be a fourteen days' notice, and notice of appeal from any interlocutory order shall be a four days' notice.

4. The Court of Appeal shall have all the powers and duties as to amendment and otherwise of the High court, together with full discretionary power to receive further evidence upon questions of fact, such evidence to be either by oral examination in court, by affidavit, or by deposition taken before an examiner or commissioner. Such further evidence may be given without special leave upon interlocutory applications, or in any case as to matters which have occurred after the date of the decision from which the appeal is brought. Upon appeals from a judgment after trial or hearing of any cause or matter upon the merits, such further evidence (save as to matters subsequent as aforesaid) shall be admitted on special grounds only, and not without special leave of the court. The Court of Appeal shall have power to draw inferences of fact and to give any judgment and make any order which ought to have been made, and to make such further or other order as the case may require. The powers aforesaid may be exercised by the said court, notwithstanding that the notice of appeal may be that part only of the decision may be reversed or varied, and such powers may also be exercised in favor of all or any of the respondents or parties, although such respondents or parties may not have appealed from or complained of the decision. The Court of Appeal shall have power to make such order as to the whole or any part of the costs of the appeal as may be just.

6. It shall not, under any circumstances, be necessary for a respondent to give notice of motion by way of cross-appeal, but if a respondent intends, upon the hearing of the appeal, to contend that the decision of the court below should be varied, he shall within the time specified, in the next rule, or such time as may be prescribed by special order, give notice of such intention to any parties who may be affected by such contention. The omission to give such notice shall not diminish the powers conferred by the act upon the Court of Appeal, but may, in the discretion of the court, be ground for an adjournment of the appeal, or for a special order as to costs.

8. The party appealing from a judgment or order Shall produce to the proper officer of the Court of Appeal the judgment or order or an office copy thereof, and shall leave with him a copy of the notice of appeal to be filed, and such officer shall thereupon set down the appeal by entering the same in the proper list of appeals, and it shall come on to be heard according to its order in such list, unless the Court of Appeal or a judge thereof shall otherwise

direct, but so as not to come into the paper for hearing before the day named in the notice of appeal.

11. When any question of fact is involved in an appeal, the evidence taken in the court below bearing on such question shall, subject to any special order, be brought before the Court of Appeal as follows:

(a) As to any evidence taken by affidavit, by the production of printed copies of such of the affidavits as have been printed, and office copies of such of them as have not been printed:

(b) As to any evidence given orally, by the production of a copy of the judge's notes or such other materials as the court may deem expedient.

15. No appeal to the Court of Appeal from any interlocutory order, or from any order, whether final or interlocutory, in any matter not being an action, shall, except by special leave of the Court of Appeal, be brought after the expiration of fourteen days, and no other appeal shall, except by such leave, be brought after the expiration of three months. * * *

ORDER LIX.

Divisional Courts.

1. The following proceedings and matters shall continue to be heard and determined before Divisional courts; but nothing herein contained shall be construed so as to take away or limit the power of a single judge to hear and determine any such proceedings or matters in any case in which he has heretofore had power to do so, or so as to require any interlocutory proceeding therein heretofore taken before a single judge to be taken before a Divisional court:

(a) Proceedings on the Crown side of the Queen's Bench Division;

(b) Appeals from revising barristers, and proceedings relating to election petitions, parliamentary and municipal;

(c) Appeals under section 6 of the County Courts Act, 1875;

(d) Proceedings on the revenue side of the Queen's Bench Division;

(e) Proceedings directed by any act of Parliament to be taken before the court, and in which the decision of the court is final;

(f) Cases stated by the Railway Commissioners under the Act 36 & 37 Vict., chap. 48;

(g) Cases of *habeas corpus*, in which a judge directs that a rule *nisi* for the writ or the writ be made returnable before a Divisional court;

(h) Special cases where all parties agree that the same be heard before a Divisional court;

(i) Appeals from chambers in the Queen's Bench Division.

(As to appeals from inferior courts this order provides):

10. Every such appeal shall be by notice of motion, and no rule *nisi* or order to show cause shall be necessary. The notice of motion shall state the grounds of the appeal, and whether all or part only of the judgment, order, or finding is complained of. The notice of motion shall be an eight days' notice, and shall be served on every party directly affected by the appeal entered.

16. The High court shall have power to extend the time for appealing, or to amend the grounds of appeal, or to make any other order, on such terms as the court shall think just, to insure the determination on the merits of the real question in controversy between the parties.

ORDER LXIV.

Time.

7. A court or a judge shall have power to enlarge or abridge the time appointed by these rules, or fixed by any order enlarging time, for doing any act or taking any proceedings, upon such terms (if any) as the justice of the case may require, and any such enlargement may be ordered although the application for the same is not made until after the expiration of the time appointed or allowed.

ORDER LXX.

Effect of Noncompliance.

1. Noncompliance with any of these rules, or with any rule of practice for the time being in force, shall not render any proceedings void unless the court

or a judge shall so direct, but such proceedings may be set aside either wholly or in part as irregular, or amended, or otherwise dealt with in such manner and upon such terms as the court or judge shall think fit.

2. No application to set aside any proceeding for irregularity shall be allowed unless made within reasonable time, nor if the party applying has taken any fresh step after knowledge of irregularity.

III.

SUGGESTIONS FOR THE IMPROVEMENT OF OUR JUDICIAL SYSTEM.

(NOTE.—These suggestions deal with the subject in rough outline only. They do not attempt to work out details. Moreover, they do not apply to the system of Justices' Courts. That vicious system needs separate treatment.)

Superior Courts

Provide by constitutional amendment as follows:

Transfer the jurisdictions of the Court of Errors and Appeals, the Supreme court, the Circuit courts, the Court of Chancery and the Prerogative court to one SUPREME COURT, consisting of,

An APPELLATE DIVISION,

A LAW DIVISION,

A CHANCERY DIVISION.

(1) The Appellate Division to have not less than five nor more than seven judges. They should sit in no other court or division.

Give it the appellate jurisdiction which is now exercised by the Court of Errors and Appeals, the Supreme court and the Prerogative court.

Give it all the original jurisdiction of the division or court below so far as may be necessary to enable it to completely determine any appeal and to make the order or judgment which the court below ought to have made.

Empower the legislature to authorize the Appellate Division to sit in separate divisions.

(2) The Law Division to have as many judges as may be determined by law.

This division to have the jurisdiction of the present Supreme court and of the justices thereof upon prerogative writs and upon all other matters except appellate jurisdiction on writs of error; also to have the jurisdiction of the present Circuit courts.

(3) The Chancery Division to have as many judges as may be determined by law.

This division to have the jurisdiction of the Chancellor and Ordinary and of the present Court of Chancery and Prerogative court except the appellate jurisdiction of the latter.

For the purpose of finally and completely determining any case brought in either the law or chancery division, that division to have the jurisdiction of both divisions.[1]

Subject to Rules of court, any judge of the Law and Chancery Divisions should be authorized to exercise the jurisdiction of the court to which he belongs.

Vacancies in the Appellate Division (when not filled by reappointment) should be filled by appointment from one of the other divisions.

Authorize the Judges of the Appellate Division, with the consent of the other divisions, to make temporary assignments of judges from any one division to any other.

Provide by Statute,

That, subject to rules of court, law cases be assigned to the Law Division, and equity and probate cases to the Chancery Division; and,

That the division in which a case is pending shall recognize the legal, equitable and probate rights of the parties; and that for the purpose of completely settling the controversy before it, each division may grant legal, equitable and probate remedies in the same case, or may transfer the case or any part thereof to the other division; and that, to that end, a jury may be impaneled in the Chancery Division, when necessary;

That where the rules of law and equity conflict, the rules of equity shall prevail;

That separate trials of legal, equitable and probate issues may be ordered if the court deem it best;

---

[1] The effect of such a provision as this would be to give the same jurisdiction to both divisions. I should much prefer to say plainly that one and the same jurisdiction be vested in both of them to be exercised subject to statute and rules of court. But that would be a hard proposition to the prejudices of the bar. Perhaps the form I have chosen does not much soften it.

That a jury trial be waived if not demanded a reasonable time before trial; the time to be fixed by rule.

Define a probate right as a right recognizable in a court of probate.

Authorize the Supreme court, by rules, to determine the classes of business to be heard before the Law Division, sitting in banc and the number of judges who may sit for that purpose.

Inferior Courts.

All inferior courts and their jurisdictions to be subject to legislative control, but all judges to be appointed by the Governor with consent of the Senate, as at present.

Transfer the jurisdictions of all courts of Common Pleas, Quarter Sessions and Oyer and Terminer and of the judges thereof to *one inferior court*, to be called (any appropriate name, say) the CIRCUIT COURT or SUPERIOR COURT which should have as many judges as may be determined by law.

Subject to statute and rules of court, each judge to exercise the jurisdiction of the court.

Assign the judges of this court to the counties as the demands of business may require: one or more judges to one county, where necessary; two or more counties to one judge, where that may suffice.

Transfer the jurisdiction of all orphans courts to the new court above mentioned, or, (if a separate probate court is necessary) then to one PROBATE COURT, to have as many judges as may be determined by law.

Subject to statute and rules of court, each judge to exercise the jurisdiction of this court.

If any case or any part thereof, in an inferior court, be beyond the jurisdiction of the court, let the case or such part thereof be transferred to the appropriate division of the Supreme court, on terms, by order of the inferior court or of that division.

Appeals from the inferior court to go directly to the Appellate Division.

Procedure

(1) All details of procedure to be regulated by RULES OF COURT instead of by statute, and to that end—

(a) Have one short Practice Act fixing those steps of procedure for each division which cannot be fixed rules. Put nothing in the act which can be regulated by rules.

(b) In some way, give the bar a voice in making future alterations in the rules, as is done in England. This will lessen the danger of legislative intermeddling.

(2) Require the judges of the Supreme court to hold a council at stated intervals for the purpose of recommending to the Legislature such improvements in procedure as cannot be made by rules of court.

(3) As to details of procedure—

Parties.—Adopt the best features of the English and Connecticut procedure as to parties. The principles are—

(a) Misjoinder or nonjoinder cannot defeat the action in law or equity;

(b) The court may, on terms, add, or strike out, or substitute parties at any stage;

(c) The court may proceed as to the parties before it, or may hold the cause in order to bring in parties, as justice requires. Separate judgments may be rendered for or against the parties respectively entitled or liable.

Let parties sue or be sued jointly when their rights or liabilities arise out of the same transactions or series of transactions and involve any question of law or fact common to them all; that is, when their rights depend on substantially the same evidence. But authorize the court to order separate trials, at discretion.

Adopt the English rule as to making trustees parties. (Order XVI, rule 8.)

Let married women sue and be sued without their husbands in all cases of tort as well as contract. Let husband and wife sue each other in law as well as in equity.

Joining Causes of Action.—Extend the right to do this so that tort and contract may be joined, subject to the court's control; giving it power to order separate trials of separate issues when convenience so requires.

Recoupment and Counterclaim.—Let defendant set up any cause of action whatever by counterclaim, subject to power in the court to strike it out or order a separate trial if it cannot be conveniently tried with the main action.

Process and Pleadings.—Change the form of summons so that it will notify defendant—

(a) Of the nature of the claim; and,

(b) Of the first step he should take to defend, *e.g.* to enter an appearance, or to file a pleading in defense within such a time; and

(c) That judgment by default may be entered against him if he fail to do so.

Use the same form of summons in law, equity and probate practice.

Require pleadings both at law and in equity to state concisely the substantive facts to be proved, but not the evidence of the facts.

Prohibit the prolixity now prevailing in equity pleading and in special counts and special pleas at law.

Prohibit pleading according to legal effect.

Abolish the common counts and the plea of general issue.

Abolish demurrers. Let issues of law be raised in the plea or answer, as may now be done in equity; such issues to be determined at, or before, the trial as a judge may order.

Let objections to pleadings be made on motion to strike out, or on demand for particulars, or for a more definite pleading, and be heard by a single judge.

Unless the trial judge thinks it unnecessary to do so, he should (after his verbal charge) submit to the jury in writing the disputed questions which he has stated in the charge. The questions can almost always be reduced to a few sentences. The jury's answers to these questions should be entered on the record and judgment entered thereon as on a special verdict.

Orders granting or refusing new trials should be made by the trial judge, and appealable to the Appellate Division.

The court should at all times, have power to suspend its rules in any case where justice so requires.

Append to the Rules of court a series of forms as is done in England and Connecticut. Make them concise and simple.

Appellate Procedure—Abolish writs of error. Let appeals, at law, in equity and in probate cases be taken on written notice only. Shorten the time for taking appeals.

Adopt the principle of the single appeal; that is, let appeals generally be directly to the Appellate Division.

Let appeals on points of procedure (when appealable) have precedence over other appeals, and be taken directly, on short notice, to the Appellate Division.

Let orders or judgments and decrees of court take the place of writs of mandamus, of injunction, and of the different writs of execution.

www.ingramcontent.com/pod-product-compliance
Lightning Source LLC
Chambersburg PA
CBHW020423010526
44118CB00010B/396